Comments on other *Amazing Stories* from readers & reviewers

"Tightly written volumes filled with lots of wit and humour about famous and infamous Canadians."
Eric Shackleton, *The Globe and Mail*

"The heightened sense of drama and intrigue, combined with a good dose of human interest is what sets Amazing Stories *apart."*
Pamela Klaffke, *Calgary Herald*

"This is popular history as it should be... For this price, buy two and give one to a friend."
Terry Cook, a reader from Ottawa, on **Rebel Women**

"Glasner creates the moment of the explosion itself in graphic detail...she builds detail upon gruesome detail to create a convincingly authentic picture."
Peggy McKinnon, *The Sunday Herald*, on **The Halifax Explosion**

"It was wonderful...I found I could not put it down. I was sorry when it was completed."
Dorothy F. from Manitoba on **Marie-Anne Lagimodière**

"Stories are rich in description, and bristle with a clever, stylish realness."
Mark Weber, *Central Alberta Advisor*, on **Ghost Town Stories II**

"A compelling read. Bertin...has selected only the most intriguing tales, which she narrates with a wealth of detail."
Joyce Glasner, *New Brunswick Reader*, on **Strange Events**

"The resulting book is one readers will want to share with all the women in their lives."
Lynn Martel, *Rocky Mountain Outlook*, on **Women Explorers**

SOAPY SMITH

SOAPY SMITH

Skagway's Scourge
of the Klondike

BIOGRAPHY

by Stan Sauerwein

PUBLISHED BY ALTITUDE PUBLISHING CANADA LTD.
1500 Railway Avenue, Canmore, Alberta T1W 1P6
www.altitudepublishing.com
1-800-957-6888

Extreme care has been taken to ensure that all information presented in
this book is accurate and up to date. Neither the author nor the
publisher can be held responsible for any errors.

Publisher	Stephen Hutchings
Associate Publisher	Kara Turner
Series Editor	Jill Foran
Editor	Dianne Smyth
Digital Photo Colouring	Bryan Pezzi

We acknowledge the financial support of the Government
of Canada through the Book Publishing Industry Development
Program (BPIDP) for our publishing activities.

Altitude GreenTree Program
Altitude Publishing will plant twice as many trees as were used
in the manufacturing of this product.

National Library of Canada Cataloguing in Publication Data

Sauerwein, Stan, 1952-
Soapy Smith / Stan Sauerwein.

(Amazing stories)
ISBN 1-55439-011-7

1. Smith, Jefferson Randolph, 1860-1898. 2. Skagway (Alaska)--
Biography. 3. Swindlers and swindling--United States--Biography.
I. Title. II. Series: Amazing stories (Canmore, Alta.)

F914.S7S63 2005   979.8'2   C2004-906270-0

An application for the trademark for Amazing Stories™
has been made and the registered trademark is pending.

Printed and bound in Canada by Friesens
2 4 6 8 9 7 5 3

"I'll drive the bastards into the bay."
– Jefferson Randolph Smith

Contents

Prologue

The whisky burned his throat as he swallowed, then it rode back up again on a choking belch. "I'm boss of this merry-go-round," he mumbled. Lifting his Winchester rifle from the bar, he pointed it toward the men sitting around a card table tucked at the end of his gambling parlor. "I run this merry-go-round, right?"

"Right as rain, boss," Old Man Triplett quietly affirmed, stroking his white beard. "Skagway's your town."

"Then why don't those sons-of-bitches go home?"

"They're fired up." Reverend Bowers was sitting at a table with his feet propped on a chair, facing the open front door. He spoke in the direction of a mob of miners milling in the black mud on Broadway Avenue outside Jeff Smith's Parlor. "Give up the poke. That'd be my advice. There'll be a flood of gold comin' down the Trail this time next month anyway."

"Sons-of-bitches!" Soapy Smith roared at the miners. "Take yourselves to bed!"

"Why won't you just give Stewart his god-damned poke and be shuck of all this?"

"On principle!" Soapy slammed the rifle back to the bar. "Four days ago the governor was shaking my hand!" He rubbed his forehead to ease the alcohol-induced throb. "My hand." His

voice trailed to a whisper.

"Give it to 'em boss."

Soapy lurched toward Bowers and pounded the bar. "Any man who makes a move to return that gold will get his ears chopped. You hear me?"

The men in the bar stiffened. Soapy never drank. Not like this. There was no telling what the usually affable con man might do under the influence of so much strong drink. Thankfully, Slim Jim Foster, a curly-haired youth, burst into the saloon and saved them from finding out.

"Saportas gimme this," Slim Jim said, breathless. He'd just run up from the docks. Jim slid the folded scrap of paper on the bar toward Soapy and backed away.

Soapy read the note and then, with an odd chuckle considering the tense circumstances, slowly folded it up again. "I'll drive the bastards into the bay!" Soapy checked his revolver for bullets. "It's that overfed Frank Reid who's behind all this. Time he got a taste of my temper." Soapy stuffed a handgun into a holster at his hip, reached for his Winchester, and stomped to the door.

The men in the bar waited until he'd disappeared.

"We best skeedaddle," Triplett said. He gulped his drink and stood up. "I'm thinking the Trail is the safest place about now."

Jim nodded. "Think they'll hang us?" The young man was terrified.

"Ah hell, we should'a been hanged a long time ago."

Chapter 1
From Saddle to Scam

ust 16 years old, wrangler Jefferson Randolph Smith Jr. had already been chewing trail dust for months. He'd clucked, whistled, and cajoled mean-spirited longhorns from Texas all the way to Kansas alongside his best friend, Joe Simmons. He'd driven those cattle across the Indian Territory north of his home state and forded six major rivers, with thousands of the nasty sagebrush survivors fighting him every step, in order to reach the rail terminals in Dodge City and Abilene. He hated it. But cow punching was the only job he knew.

Jeff Jr. was the eldest in a family of four, born to a slave-owning lawyer and his wife, a celebrated southern belle, on November 2, 1860. That put the boy among the privileged Dixie gentry who claimed descent from a line of affluent southern forebears before the American Civil War. Jeff Jr.'s destiny was to be a gentleman and, until the age of 10, he enjoyed that cultured status. But his father practised law without distinction in Noonan, Georgia, and put any wealth he gained into the acquisition of slaves who could work his land. The folly of that business strategy was obvious.

Once the South surrendered to the North on April 9, 1865, Jefferson Randolph Sr. was forced to farm his land himself. Until then he'd always relied on his slaves and slave-masters to run his business. He didn't really know how to farm, and besides that failing, he was never sober enough to do it properly. His lack of real experience quickly put the Smiths in a tight spot financially. For the family's survival, wiry young Jeff had to assume the farm management responsibility, and despite his age did it surprisingly well. The boy was a hard worker and, as it turned out, practically a farm management prodigy. He worked alongside the hired hands with all the strength of an adult, and directed his father's farm operations with a maturity that went far beyond his years. The fact that his young son became the breadwinner in the family may have injured Jeff Sr.'s pride. Perhaps it was the unpopulated west that called to him, but in 1875, Jefferson Randolph Sr. decided to move his family to Temple, Texas, with all they owned strapped to a wagon.

The life the Smiths found in Temple, where no one needed a lawyer, turned out to be worse than it had been in Noonan, Georgia. Before long, the family had to move again.

This time it was to Round Rock, a growing community north of Austin, Texas, which was surrounded by corn, buffalo, and free-range grazing longhorn. Jeff's father tried to practise law there and the children went back to school, but in Round Rock the Smiths were little better than lowly working class. Jefferson Randolph Sr.'s alcoholism made his law practice a bust. To feed the family his mother took a job managing a two-storey frame hotel and Jeff, now a strapping 16-year-old, got himself a job working as a delivery boy for a general store. He also took a second job as a "runner" for the hotel.

Jeff's Dixie background had given him a genteel manner. He had a soft southern accent that dripped with sugary sincerity. As a runner, it was his task to meet the trains and steer newcomers towards his employer's businesses. For every new customer he introduced at the store counters, he was paid a fee. He developed a glib banter so convincing he could fill the hotel with guests almost effortlessly. New visitors would happily follow the young lad with curly brown hair and grey eyes while he recited Shakespeare or gave reports of the latest town gossip. Jeff loved getting compliments for his recitation and would proudly puff his chest more for that than for the tips he received. "I can straighten out Greek hexameters with the best of them," he'd say, and proceed to conjugate verbs at random just to prove his point.

But hawking hotel rooms for small change didn't offer much opportunity. He wanted a chance to earn real money. And, as his friend Joe Simmons pointed out, in Round Rock that meant working in the thriving cattle trade.

More than six million cattle were trailed out of Texas in the years following the Civil War. The former Spanish territory had more free-ranging cattle than people, and since the 1840s ranchers had been experimenting with cattle drives to move their beef from scrub-pocked Texas to slaughterhouses in the east and north. They moved them to Shreveport and New Orleans, tried to drive them to California's frontier forts, and pushed them north toward the borders of Missouri and Kansas. By the mid-1860s, as the Civil War was raging in the eastern states, an Illinois livestock dealer saw huge profits if the two-dollar longhorns could be moved from Texas to booming markets in Chicago and from there to hungry soldiers' bellies.

Joseph G. McCoy established a cattle-shipping terminal in Abilene, Kansas, where the Kansas–Pacific Railroad could efficiently transport the cows to market. An Indian trader named Jesse Chisholm forged a trail across Indian Territory to the Red River. Texas drovers used that trail until the Atchison, Topeka and Sante Fe Railroad created a closer option with a cattle terminal at Dodge City. Cowboys in the thousands rode that trail until the mid-1880s, when barbed wire started stitching open range, the market became glutted, and the eastern public began demanding a better grade of beef than the drought-toughened longhorn.

With Texan playmate Joe Simmons as his teacher, Jeff learned saddle skills and practised with his six-shooter.

Natural dexterity and excellent hand-body co-ordination quickly made him as capable as any drover in the saddle, and he became adept with a firearm as well. When a chance presented itself, Jeff passed on the family responsibilities to his younger brother, Bascom. Then, with Joe, he took a job as nighthawk for one of the passing trail herds. A nighthawk, the lowest rank of cowboy on a cattle drive, was responsible for herding the drovers' horses overnight. It was an easy job because the horses were usually exhausted by nightfall.

After their first cattle delivery to the stockyards in Abilene, their reckless youthful curiosity led Jeff and Joe into the gambling halls and prostitutes' cribs. Jeff discovered he had a dark side. This included an addictive attraction to women of loose virtue and to cards. His urge to gamble was especially difficult for him to control. In Abilene, it didn't take long for him to notice that the men in dark suits and white shirts always seemed to come up winners. Jeff concluded it was because they were cheating. So, using a deck of his own, deftly marked with his thumbnail, Jeff perfected his own cheating system and practised on Joe during their return trip to Texas for more cattle.

That ride took them to San Antonio, the biggest city Jeff had ever seen, and fatefully to the circus that was in town. After a celebratory visit to a San Antonio saloon, Jeff slapped as much of the trail dust as he could off his dungarees, gave himself a good dunking in a horse trough, and followed the crowds to a group of tents pitched at the edge of town.

Locals were milling about the big top, gawking at the elephants and acrobats. But Jeff was attracted to a noisy crowd gathered under the tent ropes near the entrance. Standing behind a folding table, a man was sliding three walnut shells in a confusing pattern of circles and shifts. One of the shells hid a tiny pea, and the carnival hawker was inviting the crowd to lay a wager on which shell held the pea. All the while, he spouted a running dialogue spiked with jokes and humorous stories.

With every penny he owned in his pocket, Jeff elbowed closer to watch. The man's banter was hilarious and the young man could see that while it was entertaining, the humour was a clever way to distract the gamblers. "I can beat him at that game," he thought to himself. He eyed the moving shells carefully, concentrating on the man's hands and ignoring his words. When Jeff felt certain he knew where the pea was located, he dropped some money on the table.

"That one," he said, pointing at a shell with assurance.

Clubfoot Hall, the spieler, scooped up the money immediately. "Now son, you look like you're an observant sort and able to navigate to the privy in the dark, but you should know the hand is quicker than eye." He lifted the shell Jeff had picked. Nothing. "Tell you what," Hall continued, returning Jeff's cash to the table after exposing the pea under another shell, "you double your wager and I'll give you the first guess free."

Jeff happily did as he was told. He leaned in close to

watch the shells. Again, his guess was wrong, but this time Hall pocketed the cash.

"I think you need spectacles, son," Hall said, turning to another customer. "But you saw where it was, didn't you, sir? Why don't you give it a try? See if I lie."

Jeff peeled more bills from his wad. "Hold your horses. I'm not finished yet."

Hall put his hands to his hips and gave the boy an appraising glance. "He's downright serious, ain't he folks? What do you say?"

The crowd encouraged Jeff to try again.

"Here's five dollars." Jeff crossed his arms and stared, unblinking, as Hall manipulated the shells. Again he chose the wrong one.

"Now ain't that a shame, but it's just a game. Win or lose it's all the same." Hall lifted the greenbacks from the table with two fingers and tucked them, with the others he'd already taken, into the pocket of his vest. "Double that and I'll go half as slow. What do you say, cowboy?"

Jeff considered, and peeled off more money. Half the stake that was to carry him for the trail ride back north was already gone, but this time he felt lucky. "Half as fast and you got a bet."

Hall pinched the brim of his Bowler hat and eyed the bills the boy had slapped onto the table. With exaggerated slowness the spieler exposed the pea and then rhythmically mixed up the shells. When he lifted his hands from the table,

Jeff pointed to a shell. The boy was confident this time and his choice got general agreement from the rest of the crowd.

"You sure? That pea jumps around like the flick of a lamb's tail."

"Damn sure," Jeff answered, not lifting his eyes from the shell he'd chosen.

"Well, I'm going to give you a chance in a million my young friend. A chance to win it all back. You double that bet there and I'll let you pick twice. How can you go wrong?"

The crowd egged Jeff on until he finally agreed to count out half of what remained of his pay. Hall turned the first shell. Nothing. Then the second. Nothing.

"Now ain't that a shame. Just a shame. But you need specs, son. Anybody can see this one holds the pea!" Hall lifted the third to expose the withered green seed.

Jeff couldn't believe his eyes. He'd been certain! "One last time," he said, dropping the remainder of his money on the table.

"Here's a man with the heart of a lion, folks. Courage, I say." Hall's hands moved in a blur. Of course, Jeff picked the wrong one for the last time.

For two hours afterward Jeff remained at the edge of the table silently guessing. He was always wrong and couldn't understand how Clubfoot Hall always managed to be the winner. Here was another kind of gambler, he thought, and he too had to be cheating. In just a few minutes Jeff had lost the pay he'd slaved four months to earn, but he wasn't the least bit angry. The experience intrigued him. He simply *had* to learn the trick! To him, it was obvious that if he did, he could earn more money faster than he'd ever imagined, and he'd never have to sit on a saddle in a cloud of cattle dust again.

Jeff waited until Hall was ready to fold up his table.

"No refunds," Hall said, a sudden sharp menace in his voice. "*Caveat emptor.*"

"Buyer beware. I know that."

Hall looked up, surprised by the answer. The slim dirty cowboy wasn't the rube he expected. The boy's grey eyes glinted and he had a devilish grin. "I need a job."

"Talk to the ring master. He can always use another shovel behind the elephants."

"I'd rather do your kind of shovelling," Jeff said with a laugh. "Teach me the ropes and I'll split what I take down the middle."

"If I taught every sucker how I trimmed him, how long do you think I'd be in business?"

"I'll go somewhere else. There's plenty of room."

"Nope," Hall answered, "there are enough people in the shell game around here as it is." Jeff remained undeterred and pressed him again. Hall eyed the youth carefully and shrugged his shoulders. "What the hell," he decided. "The king of the shell game is up north working the camps. Fellow named Taylor. Go ask him. Every master needs a protégé." He handed Jeff the suitcase and the tripod that served as his gambling table. "In the meantime, you can carry my keister and tripe to the saloon," he said, limping away.

Jeff never returned to the Chisholm Trail. For the next nine years he wandered the western United States, allegedly chumming with reprobates like the Dalton gang of Kansas outlaws. It wasn't until 1885, when the whispers of rich pickings coming from the mountains in Colorado grew too loud to ignore, that he finally learned the secret of the shells.

Chapter 2
Soap and Suckers

During the summer of 1859, a year before Jeff was born, prairie schooners stretched like a snake of dirty dust-laden canvas across the plains. They were following the twists and turns of the Arkansas River to the base of Pikes Peak. The hopefuls in the wagons trekked west with brave determination, many painting up the flapping sides of their conestogas with the confident claim: "Pikes Peak or Bust." By that spring, news had spread across the nation of a gold strike in California Gulch. The prospectors, many of whom were farmers with families, had no idea what gold mining entailed or what challenges faced them in the quest. But it didn't matter. No river or mountain was going to stop their push up the narrow rocky gorges to the source of the yellow they prayed was waiting in the gold-bearing gravel beds at places like Tarryal Creek.

Within a year of the gold discovery, the Colorado community of Oro City, where the wagons finally stopped, blossomed from nearly nothing to a town of 10,000 inhabitants. By the time Jeff was born in 1860, however, the blush had already faded on that dream of easy wealth. The veins that supplied the placer gold continued to be a mystery in the hands of inexperienced miners, so the race to the Pikes Peak territories petered out almost as quickly as it had begun.

No one realized that the rich silver-lead ore, which covered the region like filigree, was worth mining. The nuisance of the "heavy rock" often clogged their roughly hewn sluice boxes. It had to be tossed out by hand and that only made the job of gold panning harder. The discarded ore was so plentiful it started to accumulate in huge piles. There wasn't a spot of yellow to be found, and the miners missed the significance of the heavy rock. After the rush ended, the remnants of Oro City in the shadows of Pikes Peak amounted to a few cabins, some abandoned sluices, and those pesky piles of ore.

It wasn't until 1874 that an experienced miner named A.B. Wood recognized the worth of the stacks at California Gulch. He quickly realized he was staring at mountains of lead ... and silver. Active prospecting for *that* precious metal began in 1877. A few stalwart residents in the area petitioned for a post office, asking to name their sparsely populated new home "Lead City." With just 200 inhabitants, though, the more fitting name of Leadville was approved as a compromise by the authorities.

When Jeff Smith was honing his skills as a cardsharp in cow towns across the west, sourdoughs like A.B. Wood were combing the mountains of Colorado and had finally discovered rich deposits of silver near Leadville. Soon productive mines were established, and the population of the inappropriately named community grew with the speed of a prairie wildfire.

Within three years, by 1880, Leadville boasted 15,000 inhabitants. It had 45 kilometres of streets, a half-kilometre of saloons, and more than eight kilometres of water mains. Leadville had turned from deserted to desired almost overnight. The boomtown in Lake County attracted settlers and businessmen of all kinds, and with them the usual retinue of ne'er-do-wells who followed any rush, eager to peck at miners' profits. Prostitutes, entertainers, saloonkeepers, street hawkers, gamblers, thieves, and cutthroats all swooped down on Leadville as the town grew. Among them were characters like western icon Doc Holiday, the consumptive dentist-turned-gambler; Calamity Jane, the trick-shooter and sometime prostitute; and Wild Bill Hickok, the buffalo hunter and gunfighter. Eventually, that roster also included Jefferson Randolph Smith, gambler and con man.

Jeff had become a slender, dapper-looking huckster. He had a thick thatch of black hair, and his clean-shaven face lit with a ready smile whenever he spoke, which was often.

For nine years he'd been living a nomad's life, perfecting his dexterous card manipulation with half-drunk cowboys in saloons across the frontier. He was in the habit of moving into a small town, operating his crooked poker game for only a few days, and then quickly moving on in search of fresh victims. He'd never been to a place where he could just settle in and wait a while for a stream of suckers to pass his way.

Although Leadville wasn't a lawless settlement without rules, it was still a dangerous place when Jeff arrived in 1885. Over the course of just three days, for example, Doc Holiday found himself accused of murder twice. Gunfights were almost a daily entertainment. Jeff had barely stabled his horse in Leadville when he was warned to avoid the flim-flam artist who had set up a shell game at the corner of Third and Harrison. "Old Man Taylor is trimming suckers," he was told seriously.

The name immediately rang a bell for Jeff. While his skill at poker was providing a good living, he recalled with private amusement how easily a clubfooted man had separated a certain callow youth from his cattle-drive pay in San Antonio nearly a decade earlier. Jeff decided to revisit that memory and see the man Clubfoot Hall had called the King of the Shell Game. He located him easily enough by the crowd of booted miners loudly complaining about their bad luck. A heavy-set elderly fellow, V. Bullock "Old Man" Taylor, had set up his tripe and keister on the corner and was raking in the miners' bets by the fistful. Jeff sidled to the front of the crowd and winked at the spieler.

Taylor took notice of Jeff's attire. "Texas greenbacks are as good as any," he said, inviting the cowboy to make a bet.

"Too easy," Jeff answered. "I don't want to rob an old man."

"Forget about the old man. Make your bet," Taylor challenged.

Instead, Jeff turned to the crowd and loudly announced he knew how the game was played and anyone who didn't was wasting his money. While he evasively answered questions from the crowd, Taylor silently fumed and finally packed up in disgust. Jeff followed him to a cheap rooming house and, moments after Taylor disappeared inside, knocked at his door. He introduced himself as Clubfoot Hall's friend and procceded to blackmail Taylor into divulging his secrets. The old man had little choice. If he didn't take the young cardsharp under his wing, he fully expected Jeff would haunt his shell game and chase away every sucker.

With his natural dexterity, it took only a few days for Jeff to master the sliding motions of the shell game and the palming of the pea, and then he set up shop for himself on Taylor's corner. His business attire was a clean black suit topped with a flat-brimmed stetson. His tools were Taylor's travel-worn keister and folding tripe, three shellacked walnut shells, and a dried pea, all of which he rented from the old man for a share of his profits.

For weeks, Jeff's fast-buck money machine teased

Leadville's newcomers unmercifully. The miners would gather on the street to see the tall man's amazingly dexterous manipulation of the sliding shells. When the wagering on that game dried up, Jeff simply switched to Three-Card Monte, the same scam using bent playing cards. But Jeff didn't *really* start milking suckers until Taylor introduced him to several other grifters in town and explained how to use them as shills.

Taylor's idea was laughably easy. To get the stakes up for his shell game, Jeff would play with his new cohorts. They would bet and lose, double up and lose, double up again and win — big time. To a roar of pleasure from the crowd, which always attracted even more suckers, Jeff turned over stacks of bills to his accomplices. Seeing the huckster on a losing streak, the crowd would chide and taunt. "Sweet justice!" they'd say, raining money on his keister for a chance to do the same. None of his victims, of course, ever realized it was just a way of banking the team's winnings. Jeff maintained the cordial fluid banter of a southern gentleman through it all and rarely closed shop until he'd made $200. Then, after a heavy loss to his partner, he would apologize to the crowd. "Sorry, folks, that gent just busted me out. Not even change to buy myself a meal. But try me tomorrow. I know my luck has got to change." Jeff's pose seemed honest, but his game was as crooked as they came. It was an unbeatable style as long as new suckers came to play.

After spending weeks in forced retirement, however, Taylor was getting bored. His share of Jeff's take was handsome but he was itching to earn more so he resurrected another scam he'd invented and set up shop on shipping boxes across the street from Jeff. Before Jeff realized it, Taylor's sonorous voice was stealing his crowd. Consumed with curiosity, Jeff pocketed his walnut shells and decided to take a look. Taylor had his sleeves rolled up and was displaying his elbows to the crowd. "No grime anytime with this magnificent product!" He barked with gusto about his wooden box filled with soap bars.

"What's going on?" Jeff asked an eager miner who was waving a greenback, trying to get the hawker's attention.

"Them's special soaps," the miner said excitedly. "Some's got an Abe Lincoln tucked under the paper."

A dollar bill for a chance at a five dollar bar of soap? Now that is an interesting scam, Jeff thought to himself with a chuckle, no longer angry at Taylor for spoiling his shell game. He moved to the edge of the crowd until he caught Taylor's eye, and then quickly brushed at the side of his nose with an index finger to indicate he was ready to join in Taylor's new game. With a dramatic flourish, Taylor sold Jeff a bar of soap.

"Take a look sir, and see if you are among the lucky."

Jeff peeled back the wrapper and slowly tugged out a five-dollar bill for everyone to see. "I'll be damned," he said, waving his win, "give me five more!"

"Not on your life!"

"Me first!"

Taylor sold all his soap in under a minute. Of course, none of the new customers found anything under the wrapper. Jeff was impressed with how quickly Taylor had pushed his soap and realized he could improve upon the scam with some simple adjustments in style.

The next day, Jeff purchased enough five-cent soap bars from the dry goods merchants in Leadville to fill his keister. Then he visited the Leadville print shop and ordered up the printing of new soap-bar wrappers, stamped on bright blue paper.

That evening, Jeff explained just how he was going to add a little dazzle to Taylor's scam. He removed the wrapper from one of the bars he had bought earlier and replaced it with his own blue version. "Let me introduce you to Sapolion ... the best soap money can buy," he told Taylor. He held up the bar. "Take a good look at what's going to turn us into the richest grifters in Leadville. Cleanliness is next to godliness. With Sapolion we'll wash out every wallet in town."

The following afternoon, Jeff set up his keister in a different location. His shills went to work as they always did, trying to gather a crowd. But this time, instead of coaxing players to the shell game, they touted a chance at free money. Fatty Gray, a gargantuan 300-pound man, was given the job to "set" the game in the busiest saloon in town. Fatty spent an hour that morning rubbing dirt over his exposed skin and clothes to fit the role of a thirsty miner who appeared to have just arrived in Leadville. Old Man Triplett, a septuagenarian grandfatherly type, dug out two canes from his costume trunk and stationed himself on a bench across the street from where Jeff would be "performing." Jeff took the morning to visit the barber. He also bought himself a new black suit, a fine wide-brimmed black hat, and a glistening silver watch chain. That was how Jeff wanted to appear to his customers, more like a lawyer than a street hustler.

In the afternoon, Fatty began to build a crowd of suckers in the saloon. He took a position at the bar and, after drinking a few tall glasses of beer and idly kibitzing about mining, made a loud inquiry about a bathhouse. Then, without further fanfare, he peeled the bright blue wrapper from his new bar of soap as if getting ready to go for a good soak. Instead of leaving, however, he shouted for joy at an apparent surprise under the wrapping — a $100 bill. With whoops and hollers he hurriedly explained where he'd bought the soap and proclaimed his amazement at learning there were still honest men alive in Leadville. The soap salesman had told the truth, he exclaimed! Some of the bars in his case *did* have money under the wrappers.

Fatty's acting literally pulled the saloon patrons from their chairs. Before long the miners, with Fatty in the lead pointing the way, were elbowing their way to the corner where Jeff was standing, ready to start business.

"Right there I tell ya! He's the one who sold me the soap!" Anxiously, the buyers Fatty had corralled formed in a half-moon around Jeff.

"I am that man," Jeff shouted. "I am indeed the only man in Leadville with Sapolion! This is a soap made in my own laboratory from a secret formula. Use this soap to wash away your sins!" Jeff held the bars high in both hands. "Cleanliness. It's next to godliness but the feel of a crisp $50 in your pocket is paradise. Step up, my friends, and watch me carefully. If you want to take a chance on winning one of these little papers with the big numbers."

Jeff waited for Triplett to whack his way through the crowd. "You sayin' there's money in every bar?" Triplett pointed at Jeff's keister with one cane.

"No, sir, I am not." Jeff tossed one of his bars into the suitcase and peeled open the wrapper on the other. "Just a few but a few more than you'll see anywhere else." Jeff showed the crowd a $50 bill, slid it next to the soap, then he refolded the wrapper and mixed it in among the rest of the bars in his case. "For the ridiculous price of only five dollars, gents, I'll let you buy my soap. Just five dollars for a chance to get rich quick."

Triplett laid his canes across the keister and pulled out a worn wallet, secured to his belt with a chain. "Well, you're a darn fool, young fella. I seen you put it in there so I'll buy that chance." With the support of bystanders to hold him steady, Triplett carefully rooted among the bars looking for the one Jeff had marked with a corner tear. To the crowd's amazement, he opened his bar to expose the $50 bill.

"There you have it, gents. The wisdom of this old-timer has proven my veracity. For just five dollars this lucky fellow bought the best bar of soap in all of Leadville. Give it a try. Take a chance. Even if you don't find the lucky bar, you've just bought yourself the finest soap ever made and worth every nickel. Now watch me close, gents."

This time Jeff folded a $10 bill inside a wrapper, sealed it carefully, and mixed it in with the rest of the bars in his suitcase. His soap stock disappeared in a flurry of sales.

Taylor went back to his shell game while Jeff's refinement of his soap scam worked its miracles in another part of Leadville for weeks to follow. The trio of con men was careful to mount their scam only once a day and only when the fresh faces outnumbered the locals. It continued until an easterner, who'd spent nearly $100 in a pitiful attempt to win, complained. Jeff's Sapolion stand had to be packed up after the con man was seized by the Leadville sheriff on charges of flimflam. The sheriff, responding to the easterner's complaint, had peeled back every bar in Jeff's case and, of course, found no hidden bills. Jeff was summarily marched to the Leadville jail with a crowd of disgruntled soap buyers in noisy pursuit talking about feathers and tar. The sheriff was so flustered by the crowd's anger, he forgot Smith's first name when he went to register the arrest. He completed the easterner's formal complaint by scrawling "Soapy" instead of Jefferson.

The branding with the new moniker made it impossible for Jeff and his shills to mount their scam again in Leadville.

Though he was disappointed at the turn of events, Jeff felt ready for bigger things anyway, and he and his confidence men quietly left town. He'd learned a few lessons from his experience, the most important of which was to guard his freedom at any cost. To do that he needed a real gang that could shield him from the pestering attention of the law.

He moved to Denver to build himself one.

Chapter 3
Marks, Mayhem, and Sure-Thing Men

hen gold mining frenzy formed the mile-high city of Denver, Colorado, the glee club of businessmen who had settled there were predicting a thriving metropolis of 100,000 people before the end of the century. By the 1860s, however, it looked like the boom had already gone bust. The census taker found only 34,000 people in all of Colorado in 1860, the year that Soapy was born. By 1889 the city was entering an economic depression. The growth that had been brought by mining collapsed in the 1890s, just as Soapy Smith, Fatty Gray, and Old Man Triplett swaggered into town.

Soapy set up shop on the corner of Seventeenth and Larimer Streets, a high-traffic area of town. In the evenings, he moved to Holladay Street, then the centre of Denver's red-light district. Finding targets for his Sapolion pitch was much more difficult in Denver than it had been in the wild, free-spending atmosphere of Leadville, but in a way the economic collapse surrounding Soapy was a perfect environment for other reasons. Soapy identified an untapped resource for con men happy to accept him as their leader, men who were as down on their luck as the high-flying mining promoters they'd been cheating for years. Prominent among the tricksters Soapy found were Charles "Doc" Baggs and "Canada" Bill.

Baggs was one of the most notorious skin-game artists in the frontier. He'd begun his career as a Three-Card Monte steerer, a man who herded victims, like a drover did cattle, towards a partner's Monte game. He claimed to have been arrested "about a thousand times" but never convicted. On one occasion, when charged with bunco-steering, Baggs defended himself and demonstrated the guile for which he was famous.

"Gentlemen," he'd told the court, "no such term as 'bunco-steerer' appears in the statutes defining criminal acts. How could I possibly be guilty of a charge not prohibited by the statutes?" In his argument for innocence he'd produced a thick dictionary and had defied the court to find the definition on which he'd been arrested. The baffled judge couldn't, so he'd dismissed the case.

Soapy's *modus operandi* was to go for volume in his scams, and get a little bit from a lot of victims. Baggs's style of flimflam was to find a rich victim and take him for a big loss. "I defy the newspapers to put their hands on a single man I ever beat that was not financially able to stand it," he once declared. "I am emotionally insane. When I see anyone looking in a jewelry store thinking how they would like to get away with the diamonds, an irresistible desire comes over me to skin them. I don't drink, smoke, chew, or cheat poor people," he said proudly.

But if you were a rich social climber, you were a target for Doc. He was always among the best dressed in a fancy-dressed crowd, and he was a consummate actor as well, which made him a perfect addition to Soapy's entourage. After dipping into his impressive costume wardrobe and his case of disguises, Doc could be just as convincing playing a rancher or miner as he could a banker or minister.

Among Baggs's more famous confidence tricks in Denver was the Gold Brick Game. With metallurgical skill, Baggs coated a lead brick with a sheen of gold and then went about fleecing wealthy and prominent business leaders. He would spin a story of how urgent debts were forcing him to sell the brick at a pitifully low price or how the brick had been stolen from the Mexican treasury. Among his victims were a U.S. senator and a mine company president, who each paid $25,000 for their phony brick. He was also able to con a bank president out of $100,000 with the same incredible story because he paid attention to detail.

Baggs operated his scam out of an office with an

ornately decorated waiting area. When visitors entered, they were treated to a distant view of a huge desk and a safe that appeared to be no less than two metres wide. Baggs would seat his visitors in a comfortable leather chair so they could sneak a look beyond the massive safe doors that appeared to have been accidentally left open. "Appeared" was the key word. The desk and safe were actually only images on a cleverly produced painting. After a sucker was trimmed, the desk and safe were rolled up and the office quickly transformed. If victims returned with the police, all they found was a plainly furnished woman's boudoir. Baggs chose targets he recognized as greedy, the so-called pillars of the community who were secretly willing to take advantage of an out-of-luck businessman. When the targets discovered the truth, none were willing to expose their shallow characters or suffer the embarrassment that would ensue when it was known they had been fooled.

Canada Bill's exploits were more mobile than Baggs's, and his swindling schemes were often news sensations. He was a master of disguise, and of cheating at cards. He continually operated on trains running between Colorado and Chicago, swindling passengers at will. Despite the concerted efforts of railway detectives, he was never caught and became one of the Pinkerton Detective Agency's "most wanted" men. Even when a victim's squeal of dismay was immediate, in only the time it took to move to another passenger car, Canada Bill could switch disguises.

The audacity of Baggs's confidence games and Canada Bill's incredible sleight of hand greatly impressed Soapy, and he vowed to someday do just as well. He was learning more every day, and he picked up a superstition from Canada Bill that would follow him the rest of his life. Bill was heartless when it came to skinning train passengers. His favourite habit when leaving a train was a bet with his shills. "Fifty dollars to fifty cents you can't find a ten in that entire caravan — outside of a silk stocking." But if fate put someone in distress on his path, Bill would go out of his way to help, and would do so generously. It had to come about in the course of circumstance, but when it did he called it "Bill's Luck." He believed the opportunity was a gift of fate that would return to him a hundred-fold. And Soapy bought right into it.

Some of Denver's resident grifters laughed at Soapy's age and his look of apparent innocence when he invited them to join his gang. They had always tried to blend with the population, but Soapy took precisely the opposite tact. He grew a heavy black beard to look more mature and donned a new sombre black suit, a pair of polished boots, and a diamond stickpin in his cravat. To build his reputation, he made it obvious he was an easy spender. He tipped newsboys five dollars for a paper or ten dollars for a buff of his already gleaming boots. If he couldn't impress the con men with tales of his Leadville flimflams, he knew he could attract them through their greed. And it worked. Soapy drew some of the most notorious grifters in the west to his fold.

Jefferson "Soapy" Smith

There were others in his expanding gang with less impressive credentials, of course, but each had special talents just the same. Icebox Murphy, for example, aspired to be the greatest safecracker in the United States. He had earned his nickname after accidentally blowing a meat locker instead of a safe in a butcher shop.

As Soapy acquired his retinue of crooked dealers, card-sharps, and bunco artists, he took advantage of Denver's depressed economy to protect himself from the law, just as he'd planned. His newly chosen profession was not considered criminal per se, but it floated very near illegality. Soapy made a point of ingratiating himself with the authorities. He liberally spread his money to any lawman with an open hand, and through his connections in law enforcement was always ready to come to the defence of a gang member caught in the act. He paid their fines, hired their lawyers, and spread graft on their behalf with such loyalty that no one in the gang ever doubted whose side Soapy was on.

On most evenings, Soapy was a regular at the faro table in the most notorious saloon in town. Murphy's Place had gained the infamous title of The Slaughter House because of the drunken brawls and killings that occurred there almost nightly. But during the day he held court from a dignified office in a building that overlooked the corner where he'd first set up shop on Seventeenth and Larimer. He outfitted it in fine mahogany furniture, thick rugs, and a massive side-board stocked with liquors, wines, and crystal. Discreet exits behind sliding panels were also a feature of his headquarters, through which con men and crooked cops could come and go unseen.

For entertainment, Soapy Smith made daily visits to Bat Masterson's Palace Variety Theatre as well, and on one occasion earned an introduction to Anna Nielson, an actress who sang in the footlights under the stage name of Addie. The Palace Variety Theatre was a saloon famous for its fast games and faster women. William Bartholomew "Bat" Masterson, the "gentleman lawman," dealt the cards at the faro table there. Masterson, a Canadian who was born in Quebec in 1853, migrated to the shady world of gamblers and vice from his life as a lawman. A bevy of pretty girls who dressed in revealing clothing and enticed customers to loosen their morals with expensive hootch were an added appeal for Soapy.

The day Soapy met Addie, she was in the process of singing a lusty set of ballads at the Palace. When a half-drunk bruiser decided to acquaint himself with the scantily clad singer, Soapy was outraged. He'd been secretly admiring her for weeks, so he leapt to her rescue. The fight that followed was bloody and vicious. Soapy beat the man unmercifully with the cane he'd taken to carrying. After the fight, displaying his finest southern manners, he escorted Addie to safety. Soapy showed uncommon devotion to Addie after that, reliving the cultured style he remembered seeing gentlemen exhibit with fragile southern women in Georgia. To

Soapy, Addie represented a way to demonstrate his heritage and claim social standing. He removed her from the saloon, bought her fine clothes, and housed her in a comfortable white cottage far down Seventeenth Street, away from his business. In 1886 they were married and, eventually, in that cottage Addie bore Jeff Smith's three children, including one christened Jefferson Randolph Smith. Addie maintained a household as normal and straight-laced as those of any of the Denver businessmen who were their neighbours. Few of the gang were ever invited there because Soapy was diligent about separating his private life from his business. On Sundays, Soapy took his family to Logan Park, a picnic area frequented by Denver's high society.

Unfortunately for him, however, mixing with the city's venerated citizens prompted jealousy among his cohorts. They told themselves what was good enough for Soapy was good enough for them, and on one sunny Sunday Doc Baggs led the gang to the park. What they found was a harvest of suckers with cash, the kind of victims who never frequented the seedy haunts they controlled. Perhaps thinking Soapy was keeping this bounty to himself, they reacted by setting up shell and Monte games and proceeded to fleece the fun-seeking park crowd so aggressively it resulted in a riot. Guns were drawn and shots fired. It was all too much for the good people of Denver to ignore.

The next day, one Denver newspaper, already on a crusade against Soapy's style of business, launched an attack on crime. For days, follow-up articles exposing the gang were published. Because of the furor, city hall officials considered running all of them, including their leader, out of town. Soapy reacted by telling the mayor, "No one can compel me to leave this city, and so far as exposing me, that cannot be done, because I have the utterances of all the newspapers in my own hand, and they will not use my name."

Soapy, however, decided not to push the point. To allow the controversy a chance to settle, he opted to give the gang a vacation. Almost overnight they scattered. Soapy moved his family to the resort town of Idaho Springs and then hopped an eastbound train headed for New York.

His ploy worked — partly. Before long, everyone in Denver forgot about the dangers the gang had represented. Everyone, that is, except Colonel John Arkins, a crusading newspaperman. Arkins continued to publish stories about the gang and went so far as to specifically identify Addie and the children to unsuspecting Denver socialites. He also published the fact that they were vacationing in Idaho Springs. When Soapy returned from New York he found his wife totally distraught. Through sobs she recounted how the article had prompted Idaho Springs society to snub her and the children. She declared that staying there was untenable and insisted on leaving — not just the resort but also Colorado. Soapy was livid. He put his family on a train for St. Louis and then steamed angrily to Denver to exact his revenge.

The only gang member in Denver whom Soapy could

find was a gigantic fellow named Banjo Parker, but Banjo was the only help he needed. With Banjo's 250 pounds of muscle, Soapy stationed himself on the street outside the newspaper office and waited for Colonel Arkins to emerge. Along with his gun and dagger, Soapy hefted a thick rattan cane. To the gasps of witnesses held at bay by Parker, Soapy launched a near-fatal attack on Arkins when he appeared, beating him with the rattan cane and then kicking him until the newspaperman was unconscious. His assault was so obvious that the police had no problem proving the attacker was Soapy. In just days, the crime boss was in a preliminary hearing standing next to a heavily bandaged Arkins.

The prosecution screamed for a charge of attempted murder. But Soapy argued the incident was a justified act committed by a man driven into poverty by the newspaper, a man whose respected family reputation had been unfairly smeared. The judge, perhaps a recipient of Soapy's largesse, agreed. Soapy was bound over for trial on assault charges in a district court and given release for bail fixed at a mere $1000.

Without family in Denver, however, Soapy saw no reason to stick around and perhaps face a jail term. As soon as he was free he left, certain he would never again return to Denver. The publicity over the Colonel Arkins incident made sure there was not a welcome to be had in any community near Denver. It was no better in Wyoming, which received the Denver newspapers, so Soapy and a half-dozen of his gang turned toward Utah. But disdain for gambling in the Mormon cities of Salt Lake and Ogden soon had him relocating across the border in Pocatello, Idaho. Soapy called his gang together and tried to assert his criminal dominance in Pocatello and other cities, like Spokane. But even with the threat of guns and mob-style murders, nothing matched the high life they'd had in Denver. Soapy grew homesick and despondent, so it was with great satisfaction, more than a year after he'd left, that he read letters from friends in Denver. His friends reported that the "reformers" who had worked so hard to remove him had been overcome by a more liberal lot, and that Denver was now running more wide open than ever. Instead of Soapy's relatively harmless crime style, in his absence a more physical kind of criminal element had taken over. Violent robbery was commonplace, his friends said, and businessmen were even wistfully wishing for the days when Soapy Smith controlled Denver's riffraff.

Soapy wasted no time in getting back to grant their wish.

Chapter 4
Moving On —
To Silver

Soapy had no intention of repeating his earlier experiences. This time he vowed to control the city and to ensure no one ever had the power to run him out. With his gang he quickly reasserted his dominance over the Denver underworld and then concentrated on political circles. With an army of grifters and thieves to command, he stuffed ballot boxes in the municipal elections and installed his own elected officials.

As soon as his crime network had raised enough cash, Soapy also diversified his operations from shell games and soap scams. He opened the Tivoli Saloon and Gambling Hall, and his gang of steerers made sure it was full at all hours.

Because of the Tivoli's huge profits, Soapy quickly regained his former notoriety in town. He no longer tried to lead a law-abiding private life. Instead, he flaunted his status as the crime king. To his dismay, and though he had promised Addie she could return to Denver with her head held high, his wife refused to budge from St. Louis. That soured Soapy's demeanour. To visit his family he had to travel to St. Louis, and doing so seemed to have an effect opposite to what may have been expected. When he returned from his visits, he was quarrelsome and frequently got into fights. His trips to Addie became infrequent. He took prostitutes for companions, complaining they were "the only kind of woman to be trusted." With his investment in the saloon, Soapy was transformed from a grifting buzzard who picked at his victims on street corners, to a well-dressed hawk with his own nest, always filled with suckers.

Gamblers who went to the Tivoli in hopes of winning any money made a big mistake. Soapy hired the best dealers in Denver. His roulette wheel was fixed, his cards were marked, and Soapy made no pretence about running an honest house. Over the door to the parlor he had a large sign painted that gave his saloon a high tone and also provided a warning. His advice, "Let the Buyer Beware," was written in Latin so it was completely lost on most of Denver's inhabitants.

Soapy comically referred to that sign when the Clerical Association of Denver accused him of contributing to the decline of morals. "I'm no ordinary gambler," he said. "The ordinary gambler hazards his own money in an attempt to win another's. When I stake money, it's a sure thing that I win." With that retort, new terms were added to the American lexicon. The terms "sure-thing game" and "sure-thing men" have been used to describe Soapy-type activities and individuals since that time. Another term, "mark," — a reference to the suckers he preyed upon — is also attributed to Soapy.

Among the many residents of Denver on Soapy's extensive payroll were police, bankers, and even barbers. Why he paid off the police was obvious. The bankers helped Soapy identify wealthy newcomers wise enough to protect their money in a bank vault. And the ones not so prudent could be encouraged by barbers to talk about themselves in the supposed safety of the barbershop Soapy owned.

Soapy had his steerers posted anywhere newcomers might arrive in Denver, including the train station and the stockyards. Soapy's welcoming committee always befriended new arrivals, and their first piece of advice was where to get the cheapest haircut and shave in town. The steerers would arrive with their victims at Soapy's barbershop without arousing the least suspicion that a fleecing was about to begin. When a hot towel was wrapped over the victim's face to prepare him for his shave, the sign in the window that read "Haircut 15 cents, Shave 10 cents" would be replaced by another long list of services from mustache trims to shoe shines. The cheap haircuts became 75 cents and the shaves one dollar.

While he was getting his trim and scrape, the sucker was coaxed to tell the barber about his current situation.

Should he have a full wallet, the barber would mark the victim by shaving an inverted *V* at the back of his head. It was like a neon sign to Soapy's pickpockets and steerers on the sidewalks of Denver. They could easily identify the marks in a crowd, and either lift their wallets or manoeuvre them to Soapy's gambling den for a more cordial fleecing. After the haircut and shave, the barber would calmly tell the sucker the real price of the service. Should the customer object, he'd be shown the new sign and if he then refused to pay, Fatty Gray or Banjo Parker would be on hand to enforce payment.

Soapy wasn't always able to sail around morality, however. Occasionally he was called to answer for his shenanigans. When he was hauled before the Fire and Police Commission for allegedly cheating two visitors out of $1500, the slender grey-eyed con man had to perform a little himself. And he quickly demonstrated his ready wit and dry humour. Without denying that the visitors had been bilked, Smith claimed his gambling parlor was actually an institution of education dedicated to breaking people of the gambling habit. He'd given the visitors fair warning with his sign, he said, and because of his efforts the two men who had lost their money would never gamble again. Soapy said he should be thanked for his public service instead of being vilified for his labours.

In this second Denver incarnation, the cagey con man tried to maintain the appearance of an upstanding businessman to keep the average Denver resident on his side. His actions in that regard were pure public relations genius.

Rather than be seen as a leech, Soapy went out of his way to publicly display his community spirit. He donated free turkeys to the needy for Thanksgiving and contributed heavily to church welfare programs. Soapy even allowed ministers without churches to hold their Sunday services in the Tivoli. He developed the habit of sending crisp $20 bills to needy men and widowed women at Christmas. He was always searching for a little of Bill's Luck. Every once in a while, he addressed Bible classes in his gambling parlor. On those occasions, with roulette wheels and card tables as a backdrop, the willowy con man cleverly used himself as an example of what might happen to any man who wandered from a moral Christian life.

Soapy also diversified his activities, giving them a front of legitimacy where possible. The soap scam and the Gold Brick Game had taught him that the public was always eager and willing to spend money if they thought they had a chance of getting something for free or at a ridiculously low price. Soapy simply added a twist or two, a gentle nudge of encouragement, and he never suffered guilt for squeezing the last penny from his victims.

With the depression having fallen on Denver, many gold seekers were wandering the streets, dejected and disillusioned. Usually at the end of their cash, the men were wistful about getting home. Soapy showed his compassion. He offered a solution for them by opening a railroad ticket office. Soapy's ticket office used all the promotion techniques to be found at today's travel agency bucket shops with their low-fare appeals. His technique was to advertise railway tickets to Chicago for only five dollars. For anyone foolish enough to believe the ads, Soapy had a polished crew of steerers waiting at the ticket office. When the hopeful marks arrived thinking they'd found an affordable way home, they were informed that the specially priced tickets weren't sold *every* day, but might be put on sale at any moment. In the meantime, the steerers would suggest a quiet place to wait in the back room. The back room was, of course, another gambling den where slick cardsharps quickly sheared the naïve customers of their last few dollars.

Though Denver was a city on the skids, it didn't represent a true picture of what was happening economically in other parts of Colorado. In southwest Colorado, a miner named N.C. Creed had been prospecting near the headwaters of the Rio Grande and discovered a ledge of near-solid silver. Soapy was looking for a way to expand his own fortunes and the mining boom not far from Denver was perfect.

In 1892, Soapy was at his reckless best in the untamed boomtown of Creede, Colorado. The frenzy of miners and speculators flocking there was monumental compared to tiny Leadville or placid Denver. Mines in the mountains around Creede were producing over $1 million-worth of silver every month and new miners were arriving at 300 a day. Money was everywhere and the pandemonium was perfect for a takeover. Soapy had a fat bankroll and he gathered between 20 and 30 henchmen to join him in Creede.

During the first few days after their arrival, the Soapy Smith gang circulated quietly around the dance halls and saloons, making friends and assessing the action. Soapy's reputation, rather than serving as a warning to the miners in Creede, cloaked him in a kind of celebrity status and he quickly leveraged that fame with amazing results. Soapy considered all his opportunities in the boomtown. Doors were open to all sorts of scams in this community with no law enforcement. The only impediment to fast money took the form of a single rival named Ford. Robert "Bob" Ford was a notorious small-time crook whose claim to fame had been shooting outlaw Jesse James in the back of the head.

It happened this way: Bob Ford and his brother Charlie had connived themselves into the fringes of the James-Younger gang. After the governor of Missouri, Thomas Crittendon, put up a reward of $10,000 for any information leading to the capture of the outlaw, Bob Ford decided to turn that confidence to his advantage and benefit. By November 1881, Jesse James's robbing days were pretty much over. He'd moved his wife and children to St. Joseph, Missouri, where he settled into the community under the alias of J.D. Howard. Bob and Charlie Ford decided to pay him a visit.

On the morning of April 3, 1882, the two brothers were guests in the Jesse James home. Jesse was upset over news-paper reports that Dick Liddil, one of his gang members, had been captured. By Jesse's actions, Bob Ford knew he was suspicious that his two "friends" might have had a hand in the arrest in order to claim the bounty on Liddil. Bob Ford was fearful that Jesse James would therefore suspect he was in the process of another betrayal, for the same reason. So, while James was unarmed, Ford made his move.

After the murder, Bob Ford provided a written account for the governor. "As he stood there, unarmed, with his back to me, it came to me suddenly. 'Now or never is your chance. If you don't get him now, he'll get you tonight.' Without further thought or a moment's delay I pulled my revolver and levelled it as I sat. He heard the hammer click as I cocked it with my thumb and started to turn as I pulled the trigger. The ball struck him just behind the ear, and he fell like a log, dead."

Ford had expected to be hailed a hero, but James had made many new friends in St. Joseph. Instead of glory, Bob Ford was charged with murder and sentenced by the locals to hang. But a few hours later, a grateful Crittendon commuted his sentence. Ford, however, never got the reward money he'd been promised and Bob and his brother Charlie were plagued by the cowardly deceit of the murder thereafter. Their infamous reputation hounded them — so much so that in May 1884 Charlie committed suicide. Bob, however, overcame any feelings of guilt. He lived off the money he was paid posing for photographs as the slayer of Jesse James. And he managed to open two unsuccessful saloons in and near the mining district of Creede, Colorado.

With his reputation as the murderer of the west's worst killer and bandit, and with a lot of bluster, Bob Ford had become somewhat of a kingpin in the mining camp by the time Soapy Smith arrived with his own band of bunco artists. When Ford insisted on being the one man in camp to decide which businesses would operate and how, Soapy refused to kowtow to him. The con man disregarded all warnings from Ford's henchmen and set up his soap game on Larimer Street, making friends among the miners and sporting crowd. He gained their trust because of his affable friendly nature, even though his foremost objective was always bilking them. Quietly, and without much fanfare, Soapy began hiring Ford's men from under him. When he had the strength of numbers, Soapy publicly declared that he was going to "run" Creede.

Ford, of course, was outraged at the brazen criminal takeover and confronted him. Soapy eyed the crowd of bloodthirsty spectators who clogged the street expecting to witness gunplay between the two criminals. With a suave tip of his hat, Soapy invited Ford to a private parlay out of earshot and there gave Jesse James's killer an accounting of his position. Ford was both outnumbered in guns and outmatched in savvy. "I could run you out, Bob, but that would be an aggravation and bad for business to boot. You can stick around if you behave. Your choice." Soapy suspected Ford would take a coward's route out of trouble — and he did. Emerging from the meeting, Ford reluctantly announced the two men had decided to co-operate. "Things are going to change," Soapy added. "Starting with a new saloon I'm going to build. Then I'm going to bring some law and order to this hell hole."

Soapy's construction of the New Orleans Club on Creede Avenue began immediately, in partnership with his old cattle-drive buddy, Joe Simmons. As soon as Soapy had an office he began to fulfill his second promise to Creede's inhabitants. He organized a kind of government for the camp by rigging an election the same way he had in Denver. Working behind the scenes, he was able to select the executive council and appoint all the civic officials. From the justice of the peace to the coroner, they were all Soapy's men and he, naturally, called all the shots. With this semblance of control he added some order, using his gang to provide protection for the miners with a "fair-shooting" gunslinger named Joe Light (another old friend from Round Rock) as chief of police. Of course, the government organization never interfered with any of Soapy's business enterprises.

He ruled over Creede with lofty benevolence. While the murder rate dropped, the bilking went on at a phenomenal pace. When legitimate businessmen arrived wanting to set up shop in Creede, Soapy's regime met them with open arms and help. Only those businessmen who represented no threat to Soapy's enterprises were allowed, however. Newcomers were told, "What Soapy says goes in Creede." They quickly understood the full meaning at the lavish champagne banquets Soapy regularly organized for the merchants. He was an eloquent toastmaster, and the townspeople's deference to

Soapy was obvious.

Soapy's jovial welcome for potential businesses was outshone only by his reception for old friends. Creede's dictator could not do enough for them. "Watch out for pickpockets in Creede," he'd tell them, "and don't play the games. There's no way to beat them."

When his friends arrived in town, he'd take them for walks on the streets with a conniving purpose in mind. "When the gang sees you're my friend, they'll leave you alone," he'd confide. The dapper don of the Colorado underworld had total power and the cash from his various gambling and confidence operations flowed unchecked. Had he had any instinct for saving, he would have amassed a fortune. But Soapy liked to spend as freely as he acquired. He continued to hunt for Bill's Luck by donating to worthy local causes with a great show of charity, and he gambled prodigiously at the faro tables.

While he may have been a scourge on the law-abiding townsfolk of Creede, he also came across as a God-fearing hero. With the lessons learned in Denver, Soapy never missed a chance to present his character with that false front. On one occasion, when a visiting preacher was robbed of his Sunday collection of $600 — and his trousers — Soapy stepped right in. He admonished the general populace of Creede for turning from their Christian duty. He vowed to get control of the unsavoury elements that seemed to be lurking on Creede's streets and alleys. And with commanding injunctions, he passed around his wide-brimmed black hat. Soapy seeded the contributions with a hefty amount (likely part of the preacher's original collection), and kept up his campaign until enough money had been gathered to build the first church in Creede.

Soapy was careful to present himself as a thief with honour and a protector of the locals. When a cowboy named Ed O'Kelly murdered Bob Ford, Soapy took on the lynch mob personally. After firing his two six-guns into the air over the mob, he implored them to reason. "Stand back! Let this man alone! Justice is going to be done!" Soapy helped lead the murderer to the arms of the law and for that gained even more of the community's trust as an honourable sort. He bolstered that feeling by making sure the locals were left alone and that his gang only fleeced newcomers. He was a man who remembered his mistakes, relied on his experience, and employed what he knew worked. He was an impresario of vice, a thief of both money and ideas. While the outlaws did their work, Soapy spent every free moment dreaming up new ways to steal. Not even corpses were sacred to Soapy Smith.

* * *

An enterprising Creede gambler named Bob Fitzsimmons came up with an idea he thought would make him far richer than cards ever could. Fitzsimmons had a concrete man made in Denver and then buried it in the hills near Creede where it was "discovered" by a fellow-conspirator named J.J. Dore. Dore announced his find in Creede and, with the help of several cronies and a transfer wagon borrowed from a shipping company, dug up the corpse they called "Colonel Stone." He then put it on display for 25 cents a view in the Vaughn Hotel.

The rapid clink of the silver Colonel Stone attracted quickly got Soapy's attention. He tried to buy himself a partnership in the exhibition, but when Dore refused Soapy simply stole the exhibit and put it on display in his gambling parlor. In a vacant room, Soapy had the coal-oil lamps shaded for an eerie atmosphere and promptly claimed the artifact was a prehistoric monster. As an added feature, Soapy had a barfly give a lecture to visitors on the habits of man since the days of creation and with it had Creede's miners in awe of the wonder. But Fitzsimmons and Dore were not about to let Soapy scoop their idea without a fight. They hired a lawyer and charged Soapy with theft. Smith's response was devious. He retained the same law firm to defend him, thus making a lawsuit impossible. It is likely Soapy's gang learned where Colonel Stone was made and blackmailed Fitzsimmons because, though he had a case against Smith, he agreed to settle for an equal share of the profits from the exhibition and then mysteriously left Creede.

When the curiosity of the crowd was completely satisfied, Soapy leased the display to P.T. Barnum, and when that exhibition had run its course he sold his prehistoric relic to

a man in Washington, where presumably it crumbled away
in peace.

Chapter 5
Gold! An Irresistible Opportunity

hen the news of the Klondike gold strike flashed through Colorado, Smith felt the same itch all the miners in Creede, Leadville, and Denver were feeling. This may have been partly due to the fact that practically overnight his income had dried up as the miners stampeded their way to the coast for boats that would take them to Alaska.

Wizened prospectors had predicted a gold rush in the north for decades. One, Captain William "Billy" Moore, was particularly insightful, though in the end his forecasts and preparations were only partly realized.

Moore had made and lost several fortunes in his lifetime as a sometime riverboat captain, pilot, prospector, packer, and tracker. During the Cariboo Gold Rush he'd even experimented with using camels to carry goods on paths up the Fraser River to Lillooet and the Bridge River country. He settled what eventually became known as Skagway on October 20, 1886, believing the location, at an indentation of Talia Inlet on the northern tip of Lynn Canal, would become an important access harbour if gold were ever discovered in Alaska. His nearest neighbours at the time were Natives living at Smuggler's Cove several kilometres away and a couple of traders at Dyea, five kilometres' distance along the coast. The traders, John J. Healy, a crusty old Irishman, and Edgar Wilson, his partner, were only interested in the fur trade. But that soon changed.

Moore staked a pre-emption of 65 hectares on the gravel flats above the high tide line and, with his son, J. Bernard, settled the area by pitching a tent on the east side of the Skagway River. The property was hemmed by snow-clad mountains on three sides. The glassy surface of the small fjord reflected the sawtooth peaks with mirror-like clarity on the fourth boundary. In the fall of 1887, Moore and Bernard started to build a cabin and a pier into the shallow tidal flat of the bay. The former captain also tried, without success, to raise money in Victoria for his settlement venture but only managed to acquire a modest investment through an English land promoter.

With the $1800 he did receive, by allowing the promoter to put a lien on his pre-emption, Moore bought supplies, two horses, a couple of cows, and 6000 board feet of lumber to use for buildings in "Mooresville." He hired 15 men to help him build a sawmill and operate a steam pile driver so he could extend his pier. Moore had an official survey of his acreage completed by the U.S. deputy surveyor in Juneau, Alaska, and started to clear a pack trail along the banks of the Skagway River. Then, patiently, he settled in to wait for his future to arrive.

Prospectors had already been finding their way into the Yukon from Dyea, starting in the 1870s. In 1874, George Holt managed to cross directly into the Yukon River valley over the Chilkoot Pass by sneaking past fearsome Natives who controlled the route. Not too many others got through. George W. Carmack (Siwash George), the son of a Californian "49er," was an exception. He travelled to the north on a windjammer in 1885, and took a Tagish woman as his wife. He fathered a daughter with her and learned both Chinook and the Tagish language. Thus he was never menaced on his treks into the area the Natives called *Thron-Diuck*, meaning "hammer-water," as the Indians hammered stakes into the stream there to build salmon traps.

During the summer of 1896, Carmack was prospecting in the Klondike with his in-laws — Skookum Jim and Jim's nephew, Tagish Charley — when he encountered a Canadian named Robert "Bob" Henderson at the mouth of the Klondike River. He'd previously met Bob Henderson in 1894 and he happily renewed his acquaintance with the prospector, asking about his success. Henderson had grown up in Nova

Scotia and had begun his prospecting life in the mountains of Colorado. He'd been exploring for gold on the creeks that flow into the upper Yukon River for two years without success — until that summer. In 1896, he'd found gold flecks and nuggets worth $750 on a creek he named Gold Bottom. George Carmack asked if he could also stake a claim there.

Henderson eyed Jim and Charley. "There's room for you, George, but I don't want any damn Siwashes staking on Gold Bottom." Carmack was appalled. Though both he and his relatives were insulted by Henderson's slurs, Carmack let Henderson leave their camp unharmed, and he, Jim, and Charley resolved to stake their own claim elsewhere.

Within a few days they were tramping a creek, panning as they went, and they found a small showing of coarse gold. Carmack didn't think it to be enough to get excited about, but before staking it he decided to find Henderson's claim and compare results. Spotting smoke from Henderson's campfire in the distance, the trio made their way around the highest mountain, the area known as the Dome, and came upon Henderson and his crew. They were digging down to bedrock. Carmack told the Canadian that he'd found a showing in another creek and invited him to look, but Henderson was fixated on his own claim and refused. During their visit, Charley and Jim asked Henderson if they might buy some of his tobacco but the prospector scornfully refused. It was evident that Henderson had no love for Natives. He called Carmack aside and menacingly advised him that if he should happen to find yellow he would be wise not to include his Native companions in the claim.

Carmack listened with cold anger. The racial slur against his relatives was just as much a personal insult to him. Carmack and his companions returned to their trudging exploration along Rabbit Creek, never telling Henderson the exact location of their find. They continued to have only meagre success — until August 16. That afternoon, Carmack spotted an outcropping of black bedrock above the creek. On investigating, he nearly swooned in excitement. Gold sparkled in the sunlight, lying between the flaky slabs of rock "like cheese in a sandwich." The trio staked their claims the next day and headed for Fortymile, a settlement at the confluence of the Fortymile and Yukon Rivers, where a little over a month later they recorded their placer claims on September 24, 1896.

Perhaps because of Henderson's racism, the men didn't stop to tell him of their find. Carmack was happy to tell anyone else about his discovery, though. After proudly filing their claim, Carmack walked into Bill McPhee's smoky saloon in Fortymile. It was filled with miners whose chatter and laughter seemed to roar as loud as any mountain stream. Carmack hiked up his trousers and strode to the bar, where he introduced himself to bartender Clarence Berry and ordered his first drink in a year. After downing it, he ordered another and raised his hand to call for quiet. "Boys, I've got some good news. There's been a big strike up the river." It was, in his estimation, the largest gold strike in history.

The room hushed as Carmack explained that he'd discovered the gold in a stream known as Rabbit Creek, which he'd renamed Bonanza Creek. He told the prospectors he'd staked his Discovery Claim about 24 kilometres up the mouth of the creek, less than a half-kilometre above the junction of the Klondike and Yukon River.

By the next morning, Fortymile was deserted and the Canadian gold rush was on. In just days, news spread and men moved in to stake their own claims along the tributaries of the Klondike River. Joe Ladue, the trading post owner, loaded a boat with supplies and steamed downriver near to where the Yukon and Klondike merged. There, on a flat piece of frozen swamp, he built himself another log trading post and then rafted in a sawmill. When it was situated, he laid out the beginnings of a community. He named it Dawson after Dr. George Dawson, the director of the Geological Survey of Canada. Then American prospectors, who comprised 90 percent of the miners in the area, added the word "city." All the other boomtowns they knew were "cities": Carson City, Virginia City, Dodge City, and Circle City. Dawson needed the same distinction, they said.

The news of Carmack's strike echoed up and down the Yukon River from Dawson to its mouth on the Bering Sea, all the way to its headwaters in British Columbia, 3500 kilometres away. The men arrived from every direction. By early September 1896, a dirty white tent town was sprawling between the trees near the Klondike River's mouth. Before anyone on the outside even knew of the discovery, the miners had already staked all the most likely territory. As early as that winter, claims were already changing hands rapidly. One story says a man sold his claim for $800 only to find that three years later, when the gold rush fever was peaking, the same claim was worth $1 million.

In Fortymile, a Canadian government surveyor named William Ogilvie was searching for a way to alert his superiors in Ottawa about the claim staking going on. At that time, the border between the Yukon and Alaska was still not officially determined and he worried about an influx of Americans to the territory. Ogilvie was in the process of completing a tentative boundary survey and Canada was claiming the land from the tidewater at Dyea to the Klondike. But Americans occupying the territory with settlements could undermine the country's claim.

Billy Moore delivered Ogilvie's letter to Juneau for dispatch to Ottawa, but the bureaucrats in Canada's capital paid no attention to the surveyor's concerns. In January, Ogilvie tried again with much the same result. Feeling pressure to complete his survey before a stampede of American gold seekers might change the territorial claims on the Canadian side of the Chilkoot, Ogilvie contracted Moore for a different reason. He asked the captain to provide him with the know-how for packing over wilderness trails and to build and navigate a barge that could carry supplies down the Yukon River.

He also asked Moore, who was by then 74 years old, to look for a better route over the mountains from the tidewater to the Klondike. Moore said he knew of a better route than the tortuous climb through the Chilkoot Pass from Dyea. And it led from his pre-emption property! While the surveyor and his party trekked the Chilkoot, Moore and Skookum Jim walked a little-known Native trail, 183 metres lower in altitude.

The old man followed the rocky banks of the Skagway River. The pass they hiked was over 72 kilometres long, a maze of switchbacks, hillsides, and canyons. It followed the river for some distance before it turned sharply left up a canyon to the summit of a pass. Beyond the summit, it was necessary for the men to climb still higher. It was a treacherously dangerous trail that hugged the side of Turtle Mountain. But they took it in order to avoid the swampy arms of a body of water that would later become known as Octopus Lake. From Turtle Mountain, Moore's trail descended to a place named Log Cabin and then a little further to the head of Lake Bennett. It took them longer to reach Lake Bennett than it did the survey party, but Moore claimed his route was easier than the nearly vertical climb over the Chilkoot Pass.

Ogilvie named Moore's route the White Pass in honour of Thomas White, then the Canadian minister of the interior. "Every night during the two months he remained with us," Ogilvie later recorded, "he [Moore] would picture the tones of yellow dust yet to be found in the Yukon Valley. He decided then and there that Skagway would be the entry point to the golden fields — and White Pass would reverberate with the rumble of railway trains carrying supplies." Moore's vision wasn't far from being realized.

In the summer of 1897, the Seattle *Post-Intelligencer* claimed, "Strikes seem to be rich as reported — there is plenty of gold but only the hardy or the provident can secure it." But America was filled with hardy pioneers and providence only came to those willing to take a risk. The rush was on in a matter of weeks.

Chapter 6
Skagway —
Perfect For Soapy

On July 26, 1897, the leading edge of the rush of gold seekers reached the bog that was Skagway after the snow melted. The men were aboard the *Al-ki*, the first boat to leave Seattle for the Klondike following the arrival of the steamer *Portland*. It was trailed soon after by the mail steamer *Queen*, which sailed from Seattle on July 23 and took six days to reach Moore's idyllic little kingdom.

Up to that time, the *Al-ki* had only been plying the sheltered inland waters of Puget Sound. For its trip north, horses, mules, and sheep were jammed on the forward deck of the leaky vessel and a mountain of hay and feed was piled as high as the pilot house. To accommodate the passengers, emergency bunks had been hastily cobbled together on the decks. The gold-hungry horde sprawled atop their baggage, eyeing the apparently impassable landscape as they steamed northward. They imagined making camp and organizing the transport of their goods. They also thought of ways they could get ahead of their companions to the Klondike. Most were stunned when they saw the ghost-white tidewater glaciers that poked their blue fingers into the ocean. The 3800-square-kilometre Juneau Icefield was an immense barrier reaching from Juneau to Cordova. It was 100 kilometres of ice glinting in the cold Alaskan sunlight, and it only hinted at what was waiting for them in Skagway.

But by the time the *Al-ki* dropped anchor offshore from Moore's cabin, the men aboard had forgotten their fear. A curious excitement swept over them as they plunged into the shallow sea, their animals dumped into the water close behind them. Old Billy Moore's homestead, which lay on either side of the Skagway River, was the nearest dry land and they swarmed it like ants.

It was quickly obvious that gold fever would filter out any accepted morals, honour, or decency in the stampeders when the *Queen* arrived three days later, on July 29. The captain of that steamer, James Carroll, was unfamiliar with that part of Alaska. When he saw smoke rising from Moore's cabin he dropped anchor in the bay as the *Al-ki* had done. A "committee" of some 200 men onboard joined the earlier arrivals on Moore's property above the tidal flats, ostensibly to ask questions.

Carroll politely inquired who owned the land, and if it could be crossed. Moore told him, adding that he'd been waiting for 13 years to see an ocean-going vessel such as the *Queen* make her way to his townsite. Moore welcomed Carroll's passengers and invited them to unload their outfits on his small dock and beach. He even offered to assist. His friendly attitude was a mistake.

The advance guard of stampeders from the *Queen*, emboldened by their numbers, knew there were many more boats due to arrive in just days. The muddy tidal flat would become a bustling centre of commerce overnight. Moore, for all his vision, hadn't counted on their greed. That night, the men discussed the opportunity staring at them in the scrub brush above the beach. All knew that the land was part of a squabble between the United States and Canada, and, as such, was basically free of legal control.

Without laws, it was all about strength in numbers. The following morning, the horde invaded and told Moore they didn't care if he claimed to have title to the land. As far as they were concerned, it was frontier wilderness. The old steamboat captain protested, showing them his official survey. But the men only scoffed. They bluntly told him they were jumping his claim. Moore and his son — just two against hundreds — were helpless to stop them.

In days the stampeders slashed down trees to make room for their tents and supplies. More men began to arrive and by August 12, the occupants on Billy Moore's land had changed the area into a sprawling tent city. The settlement was a motley collection of structures, from lean-to shelters to tents and rustic cabins, all swimming in mud. Pathways wandered haphazardly, weaving around stumps and bogs from one muck sinkhole to the next. Canvas-sided saloons, restaurants, and prostitutes' cribs popped up on both sides of any path wide enough to form a rut. Arguments over who claimed what plot for himself were frequent, and often turned violent. So, to gain a semblance of control over themselves, the men organized a makeshift government. Because the area was not clearly declared to be either U.S. or Canadian territory, they were able to do so. No laws of either country were applicable, and even if they were, no courts were established to give effect to the law.

Rule by committee got its start in Skagway on December 4, 1897, when the men held their first election. Seven "councilmen" were picked to "look after all matters appertaining to the welfare of the town." A.J. McKenny was chosen as their mayor. Frank Reid, the one-time schoolteacher who was by then tending bar in the tent called the Klondike Saloon, reported that he had a set of survey instruments in his outfit. Reid was therefore promptly elected the "town surveyor" and put to work laying out the new townsite. It also became his job to collect a five-dollar registry fee from anybody who wished to locate on a new city lot. No one worried about having committed a crime against Billy Moore, especially not sharp-eyed Frank Reid.

Like many of the first stampeders to arrive, Reid's past had a few shady spots. When he graduated from teachers' college in Michigan in 1873, Frank and his older brother, Dick, headed to Oregon. Frank didn't care for the teaching lifestyle and quickly changed occupations to become a construction worker. That job led him into surveying. He also volunteered as an "Indian fighter" with Mark Brown's company of Oregon Volunteers during the Bannock-Piute Indian War of 1878 in eastern Oregon. During his service for Brown's company of militia, Reid was accused of inciting Natives to fight with settlers in order to keep the volunteers busy. Frank must have had plenty of practice with his rifle because he became known as a "crack shot."

While living in Sweet Home, Oregon, in 1879, Frank Reid had proven that questionable skill in a gunfight. Apparently, the well-mannered Reid had taken exception with an unarmed man who refused to speak when asked to do so. The one-sided conversation resulted in murder charges being laid against Reid. But Reid was somehow acquitted of that crime, on the basis of self-defence. Afterwards, Reid decided to get out of town. He moved to New Whatcom (now Bellingham, Washington) where he found work on the town survey crew. It seems Frank Reid managed to keep the expensive survey equipment, as he used it later in Skagway. Perhaps he was already thinking the tools might come in handy in the burgeoning north country.

Within days of Frank Reid becoming Skagway's town

surveyor, a town made up of 3600 lots with wide streets was laid out. The ugly stockades Moore had erected for his wild-eyed cayuse horses were torn down. The emergency bunks on the decks of the *Al-ki* and the *Queen* were dismantled and sold as building lumber to the men for $300 or more per 300 metres.

Before long, more permanent saloons, hotels, stores, and restaurants were built where tents had been standing. The committee erased all records of Moorseville, changing the name of their settlement to "Skaguay," a word taken from Native folklore (later the settlement was renamed Skagway). The Natives called the river that spilled into the ocean there the *Skugun* ("the place where the north wind blows"), and said that name had been used since "the crow made the earth and the Tlingits."

As the winter's grey ceiling of clouds arrived and a dusting of new snow powdered Skagway, more and more men arrived, dotting the long bay with hundreds of craft, ranging from rusty sea-going freighters to slim single-handed sailboats. From each vessel came eager men and women. They transferred their goods to square-bowed rowboats that shuttled them to the beach, where the goods were then heaved to the gravel. Meanwhile, any animals that had been brought along on the journey, from goats and sheep to horses and dogs, were pushed overboard into the shallow waters of the cold sea and forced to make for land themselves. Arrivals could hire longshoremen, for $20 an hour, to lug their outfits to higher ground or face the possibility of loss to theft or the rising tide. If they were unfortunate enough to have timed their landing with the latter, the same help could cost them $50 an hour. Many a *cheechako*, unwise to the rhythm of the ocean, bridled at the outrageous rates and made the regrettable decision to move their mountain of belongings alone. Unless guarded onshore, the goods were pilfered while their owners waded back to rescue supplies being rapidly covered by a rising tide. There was some urgency in these attempts, as the tide often showed depth swings of nine metres or more.

Skagway was a cursing mob of men. All of them were consumed by their mission to reach the Klondike before winter set in on the high mountain passes. They slogged along the main street, which was nothing more than a river of black mud, though it was proudly named Broadway. They hunted for a meal, a diversion, or the fleeting chance of an alliance with someone who might know a little more than they did about what was in store on the other side of the ominous mountains. In spite of its survey, the town was still a scraggly mess of dwellings. Broadway featured four saloons, however, and more were being established on nearby side streets. Any flat spots not already claimed had been turned into campsites that rented mucky ground for $10 a week.

Much like Creede had been in its early days, Skagway was a lawless place just waiting for the commanding personality of Soapy Smith.

According to the December 31, 1897, edition of *The*

Skaguay News, just three months after the first arrivals there were 700 businesses and residences cobbled together in Skagway. Old Billy Moore wasn't the only landowner to be robbed by the committee of claim-jumpers. They preyed on each other and the men and women who had followed them to Skagway just as heartlessly. Because there was less land than there was demand for it, the claim-jumpers worked out a plan to resell all lots owned by any stampeder who had trekked "inside." A miner, who thought he was buying property in good faith and had built a cabin to store his goods before leaving for the Klondike, might return to find his goods in the street or missing completely, and his cabin owned by someone else.

Because of Frank Reid's survey, Moore's cabin was deemed to be located in the middle of the town's main street. The claim-jumpers offered the captain a single lot on his own property, which of course he refused. Reacting to this affront to their authority, the men elected another committee empowered to get Moore moved. The committee arrived one day at Moore's cabin with axes and saws at the ready. Moore, despite his age, grabbed a crowbar to defend his home. With his first swing he caught one committeeman unprepared, tearing off the fellow's trousers. It served to scatter the rest of them, but Moore realized he couldn't win and decided to move before the violence escalated.

To his credit, Moore didn't give up entirely without a fight. He pursued his legal ownership in the courts and, after a four-year battle, was awarded 25 percent of the assessed value of all the lots within the original townsite of Skagway. He also sold his wharf to the White Pass and Yukon Route for $125,000 and $5000 per annum for 10 years, thus making his fortune anyway.

Many of the first arrivals decided to race winter and get ahead of the coming throng that would set out for the Klondike in the spring. They travelled the short distance to Dyea and the Chilkoot or ventured towards the White Pass. Initially, the White Pass served its purpose well. The first horses that the gold seekers used were able to cover the distance with a certain amount of humane treatment. The stampeders had bought their animals at greatly inflated rates in places like Seattle, paying as much as $25 for any tired horse still breathing. But after the first parade of horses had turned the path into a muddy, treacherous bog, passage became an ordeal for them. At first, where the footing was dangerous, the stampeders unloaded their pack animals and led them over bad spots, reloading the horses on the far side. But as the rush increased, the trail deteriorated dramatically. What were narrow but navigable paths became slides of sharp rock and gravel. The horses suffered terribly. Owners, driven to a frenzy through an urgency to reach the gold fields before all land was staked, would whip them ruthlessly. If the horses stumbled and fell, they were left to die without the mercy of a bullet. Their life on the trail averaged only six weeks. The cruelty was unimaginable. The men and their pack animals trudged over the fallen carcasses in a relentless drive to the summit. In one of the worst places on the White Pass Trail more than 3500 horses perished and were left to rot. It was no wonder the stampeders gave that spot the infamous name, Dead Horse Gulch.

Those stampeders who couldn't make it over the passes during the winter joined the men who sat waiting for spring back in town. This ballooned Skagway's population to 5000 by mid-winter. Life there had an atmosphere that was part circus and part prison — the natural barriers of rock and water effectively confined the men. The worst sides of their natures were coaxed to the surface by boredom. The streets were often an impassable river of men wandering about in search of diversion. On one street they might encounter Alexis, a trained dancing bear and its Russian handler. On another street, a man selling balloons, or Billy Moore's grand-daughter being pulled about in a wagon by a yearling moose. They might encounter Peter the Apostle fighting to save souls, or a prostitute in a red petticoat. Saloons were on every corner. And at night gunshots became so common that no one bothered to investigate whether the cause was a murder or a celebration.

Englishman Monte Hawthorne stepped off the *George W. Elder*, a steamer freighting stampeders to Skagway in the winter of 1897–98, and reported that he met with grief. "Things was about as bad as they could get," he wrote, describing Skagway as "the most outrageously lawless quarter I ever struck ... It seemed as if the scum of the earth had hastened here to fleece and rob or to murder ... Might was right." He encountered a failed prospector sitting on his Yukon sled, head in his hands, mumbling to himself. "It's hell. It's hell. Multiply by ten, and that ain't half as bad as this is."

Superintendent Samuel B. Steele of the North-West Mounted Police (NWMP) agreed, describing it as "little better than a hell on earth." To the Mountie, Skagway was an unbelievably lawless place filled with the cacophony of gunshots, dance hall music, and screams in the night. "Skagway was about the roughest place in the world."

And it fit Soapy Smith like a glove.

Chapter 7
The Skinners
and the Skinned

hen Soapy made his decision to head north, he and Addie had given up any idea of reconciliation. If Addie wouldn't return to live with him in Denver, it was a certainty she wouldn't make the trek to Skagway. Soapy created a replacement for his family with his loyal gang members, and he hand-picked them for the challenges he expected in Skagway.

"Reverend" Charles Bowers was a prime example. His saintly appearance hid a heart of granite. He was a first-class steerer and also an accomplished "grip man." That meant the soft-spoken Bowers had learned all the handshakes, signs, and signals used by secret orders to identify their members. Bowers would try his library of signals until he got a response and then he was ruthless about stealing or conning anything he could from his supposed fraternal brother. Like a skilled prop master, Soapy had badges, emblems, rings, pins, and other identifying symbols collected for Bowers to use as proof of his memberships. Echoing the lessons he learned in Denver and Creede, Soapy instructed Bowers to present himself as a God-fearing Christian sort, willing to help newcomers stay clear of undesirables. Of course, Bowers would then steer them directly to Soapy's web of deceits.

George Wilder was another important member of the Klondike team. Wilder, who dressed like a banker and appeared refined, served as the advance man. He was, coincidentally, the only member of Soapy's group from Creede with the good sense to save any of his ill-gotten gains. If it had not been for Wilder's savings account, Soapy and the six men he picked would never have been able to afford their journey to Skagway.

Among the other men were Syd Dixon and Slim Jim Foster. Syd Dixon was a prosperous-looking con man. Actually from a wealthy family, Dixon had travelled the world, and on his journeys had become addicted to opium. He used his talents at flimflam to feed his drug habit but he dressed with style and was therefore a valuable member of the gang. Slim Jim Foster was a curly-haired youth. Soapy planned on stationing Foster at the Skagway docks to help arriving stampeders carry their gear into town. Naturally, Foster would lead them to Soapy's enterprises as well. Loyal to Soapy since his early days in Denver, Old Man Triplett also came along. His job was to pose as an old sourdough full of advice about the Klondike. Red Gibbs, a man with a threatening demeanour, rounded out Soapy's "travelling crew" as the heavy. They all formed the beginnings of the Skagway gang Soapy ironically called his "lambs."

In Seattle, it was nearly impossible to gain a berth on something capable of floating men and their supplies north. Some were getting rich never leaving the port city simply by gaining passage for themselves on a boat and then selling their place on the crowded decks for three or four times what they had just paid. Soapy had himself and six others to move north. In his search for transportation, he encountered "Dynamite" Johnny O'Brien, the down-on-his-luck skipper of the steamer *Utopia*.

O'Brien had a colourful history. In his better days he'd been a stocky two-fisted sailor who'd escaped cannibals, dined with Polynesian kings, and fought off Chinese pirates as he darted from harbour to harbour across the Pacific. When Soapy found him, though, O'Brien was nearly delirious with fever in a sweat-soaked bunk in Seattle, still recovering from brain surgery. A brain tumour had burst in his skull and, on the wind-blown shores of Cook Inlet in Alaska, the sea captain had been subjected to a bush doctor's rough surgery. He was dancing with death, without the cash to fuel his ship at a time when half the world was screaming to get passage north. Soapy solved O'Brien's problems with cash and the ready discipline of six men who could serve as the *Utopia*'s officers.

Using the money Soapy offered, O'Brien was able to purchase a quantity of fuel and take on a cargo of paying passengers. Unfortunately, the quality of the fuel he could afford was decidedly lacking. Just eight hours after setting out from Seattle, with the ship's engines limping to life and dying again just as quickly, the passengers tried to mutiny and turn the *Utopia* back. Soapy, however, took control with a revolver in each hand and bullied all aboard into continuing their journey. On their week-long voyage, Soapy's gang members struck up friendships with the fellow passengers, carefully making note of all the men they planned on plucking once they reached Alaska.

Soapy addressed his move to Alaska with the precision of a field commander preparing to invade. The gang moved up the coast, stopping at prospective headquarters to assess them for their opportunity value. Wrangell, a tumbledown cluster of cabins at the mouth of the Stikine River, was a possible choice in Soapy's opinion. Lawless and disorganized, it was ripe for his control, but Smith eventually dismissed it as being too far from access to the Klondike to ever attract enough stampeders. Juneau, his next stop, was too civilized and established. Skagway, however, reeling from the onslaught of thousands of would-be sourdoughs, was ideal.

He considered its location. Skagway was hemmed in by mountains that protected easy access to the Klondike on the east and the sea on the west. Once a gold seeker arrived he had no place to go but into the bush or back to civilization and would therefore be captive to Soapy's business enterprises. The only evidence of law and order was a lone U.S. deputy marshal. In spite of Alaska's rigid laws prohibiting the importation, manufacture, or sale of spirituous liquors, booze was everywhere in Skagway. And stampeders, with their inhibitions removed, were almost too easy to fleece.

The gang went to work immediately and by October had quietly established itself. The members got to know every rest stop on the trails leading from Dyea and Skagway, and they set up their shell games and Three-Card Monte scams on handy stumps or in tents. While they worked the stampeders on the trails, Soapy raised cash with his shell game in Skagway and soon settled in at Clancy's, the saloon he considered to be the best in town. Somehow, he managed to convince the owners, Frank and John Clancy, to take him on as a partner. From their saloon, while he gathered the money he needed for his partnership, Soapy was able to increase his gang strength with the river of reprobates arriving in town. He stretched his reach even further with payoffs to other legitimate businessmen already established there, including newspaper reporters, barbers, and merchants. Soapy wanted an army of informants to help him fleece the fattest lambs and he had them by the hundreds. In fact, so many townsfolk were secretly on his payroll that it became impossible for anyone to openly complain about Smith or the gang for fear their words might be overheard and quickly whispered to Soapy by an informant.

Soapy Smith

With that kind of a network, it didn't take too long for Soapy Smith's gang to acquire enough cash from their grifts and cons to finance Smith's purchase of a small 4.5 x 15-metre building on Holly Street. With a slap of paint to the false front, Soapy renamed it Jeff Smith's Parlor, stocked it with wine and liquor, and put oysters out as the main course meal. A small room at the rear of the saloon, described by the Skagway *Alaskan* as "cozy as a lady's boudoir," was just large enough for a card table and chairs. There was a door leading from the bar to a storeroom and from there to a small backyard closed in by a high fence. The fence had a secret exit through which his gang could disappear with their loot if a victim ever tried to recoup his losses. Soapy dressed up the latrine behind the gambling parlor with a large stuffed eagle. His gang of ruffians used the eagle to lure unsuspecting newcomers out back, where they could be robbed without witnesses. "Go look at the eagle" became a Skagway phrase for two different kinds of visits.

All the plunder Smith's gang managed to take from their rich victims went directly to Smith's safe. He took a 50 percent commission as the gang leader, and from it paid for bribes, legal defence, or partial payoffs to victims who complained the loudest. Over the year, hearsay about the modest saloon grew to mythic proportions. The NWMP's official publication, *Scarlet & Gold*, said that none of the 70 or so saloons in Skagway at the time compared to Soapy's "on so lavish a scale." It claimed the bar had a capacious gaming room with

Soapy Smith's saloon. Skagway, Alaska, 1898.

crap tables, roulette and faro equipment, wheels of fortune, keno, and 21 tables. It stated that a half-dozen or more versions of poker could be conducted, and that "Soapy's local wolf pack was supplemented by ladies of easy virtue, working on commission, whose task it was to encourage prodigality among the customers." A biography of another Klondike character, Mike Mahoney, said Smith's saloon had a dance floor where customers could enjoy the company of Soapy's women to the music of a five-piece orchestra. The biography even claimed Soapy had imported artificial palm trees to flank a raised stage.

While his gang victimized stampeders, Soapy did his best to front the group by presenting an image of honesty. He circulated among the Skagway business community, making friends and acquiring spies. One of the acquaintances he made was the former gunslinger Frank Reid. Soapy may have had some previous connections with this claim-jumping, town-council-appointed surveyor. Apparently, Smith was in western Oregon during part of the Indian War period, and he may have met some of Reid's relatives. However, the two men came to know each other in Skagway, and they managed to maintain a cordial sort of relationship. They were often reported to have shared a social drink together, though Smith was apparently not a drinking man. The fact that Reid called Smith "Jeff" rather than "Soapy" may have been small proof of their friendship (Smith's friends never referred to him by the uncomplimentary nickname). The two men were opposites, however, and their attitudes towards law and order were also extremely different.

Ironically, Jeff Smith supported law and order under the control of proper authority, as long as it didn't interfere with his illegal activities. Back in Creede, he had often drawn the line on his chicanery when it involved violence. But in Skagway, he paid two ruffians — Yeah Mow Hopkins and Big Ed Burns — to act as bouncers, and he never questioned how far they took their duty. Rather, Smith said the beatings they doled out to people who complained too loudly were a public service. It was better to force those kinds of people out of Skagway, he said. As for the thievery, Soapy's propaganda claimed it too was an act of public service to the town. Not only did his gang's filching keep money circulating in Skagway, it also kept the witless and naïve out of the wilderness.

Frank Reid saw through all the bafflegab laid on by Smith. He was a firm believer in action over words. If law enforcement failed, or law officers were unwilling to take action, Reid believed it was the duty of citizens to take the law into their own hands. In an odd way, the two men respected one another. Soapy was reported to have said, "Frank, there is only one man in Alaska who can get me. If I am ever got, you'll be the man who'll do it." Reid, apparently, had agreed with him.

Smith showed his attitude toward law and order by his actions as well as his speech. It indicated he had a quirky split in his own moral code. Thievery was fine, but only transients were to be victimized. He'd taken that lesson from Denver and Creede to Alaska. The permanent locals were to be left alone. During the lull in the arrival of stampeders in late December and early January 1898, just a few months after settling in at Skagway, Soapy headed outside with plans to visit his family in St. Louis and possibly his brother on the editorial staff of the *Washington Star*. He was also making the trip to recruit more gang members and prostitutes for his Skagway operations.

Soapy Smith

On the return journey, aboard the crowded *City of Seattle*, one of the passengers died in a freak accident when a heavy lamp fell and crushed his skull. The passengers, already incensed by the inhumane treatment they were receiving, banded together and were vocally threatening a damage suit against the company. Soapy presented himself as the voice of reason. With a well-placed elbow or two, he edged through the crowd on deck to the dead stampeder, claiming the man had stolen from him. He rifled through the corpse's pockets. "Now, you scum," he shouted, holding the man's wallet in the air as evidence. "If you want to stand up for a man who is a stowaway, a cheat, and bum, I'm off with you." The mob of passengers gauged Soapy's dark suit, his polished boots, and the glare of his grey eyes and backed away. He'd fooled them all with his blustery defence of right against wrong and his insinuation that evildoers always get their just deserts.

As soon as he arrived in Skagway, three days later, he faced another angry crowd. Andy McGrath was a worker on a toll road that was being built as part of the White Pass Trail. With some time off, McGrath ventured into Skagway and headed for Clancy's where he ordered himself a drink. When he paid, however, he was refused his change. It was an extra little cheat that perhaps Soapy had initiated, as it had become standard practice that winter in Skagway. McGrath didn't think that was kosher at all. He argued until the saloon-keeper, John Edward "Ed" Fay, tossed him out. McGrath, only earning a labourer's wages in a town that was flowing with grubstake cash, wouldn't let the theft of a few coins pass uncontested. He charged from the saloon and tracked down U.S. Deputy Marshal John Rowan to demand justice. Rowan was less than enthusiastic to help. At the time, he was on a hunt of his own, looking for Dr. J.J. Moore to attend his wife, who was about to deliver the first child to be born in Skagway. However, when McGrath pressed his demands by asking to borrow Rowan's revolver, the deputy marshal agreed to help him.

When the two men entered the saloon, Ed Fay stood ready. He was expecting that McGrath might make good his parting threat to "come back and take care of things." Fay shot them both before either man could say a word. McGrath died instantly and Rowan was mortally wounded. As the deputy marshal lay dying, Fay ran away in fear. Within minutes, a lynch mob began searching the alleys of Skagway, and was moving through town swinging a rope. Soapy was quick to act. He braced the mob with his revolvers, claiming to represent the God-fearing saloonkeepers of Skagway. "We muster upwards of two hundred men with guns," he warned them. "And if anyone tries to put a rope over Ed Fay's neck he'll get a bullet in his own head mighty quick."

"Lynching doesn't go on here," Soapy shouted. "How do you know this man deserves to hang? We will let the law take its course and I personally will see that Fay gets a fair trial." The crowd dispersed. Without Deputy Marshal Rowan as their protector, the closest thing to "law" was the barrel of Smith's gun.

Fay surrendered himself the next day, probably at Smith's behest since the barkeeper was hiding with some of Smith's gang members. He declared he had shot the men out of fear for his own life. A mass meeting of the outraged miners was called in the Union Church. Soapy infiltrated the meeting with his own men who suggested to the crowd that perhaps the shooting wasn't as cut and dried as everyone suspected. The miners had to agree, and in a show of democratic zeal, they elected a committee of 12 men to investigate the murders further. In the meantime, Fay was taken out of harm's way to Sitka to stand trial. He was eventually given a light sentence. Jeff Smith was the first contributor to a fund for Rowan's widow and he diligently pressed others to follow his charitable example.

The vigilante action by the mob showed Soapy that a firm hand was necessary in Skagway, if for no other reason than to protect his business interests. He announced that, as the area lacked a policeman, he was taking control to restore law and order in the community. He had championed rationality over violence and used diplomacy with the mob. Thus, a number of Skagway businessmen came forward to support him.

Frank Reid viewed that as the fox guarding the chickens. Reid's closest friends, who had been police officers and Indian-fighters, agreed. Major J.M. "Si" Tanner and Captain J.L. Sperry stepped up to Reid's side. A number of miners who'd suffered loss through one or another of Smith's cons did so as well, and the group of them, calling themselves The

Committee of 101, opted for citizen action instead.

The committee appealed to Washington to send troops to Skagway to enforce military control. When Smith learned the infantry had been dispatched, he quickly dispersed his gang to the trails, where they could blend in with the stampeders. The military arrived, only to find that all the confidence men and gamblers had fled. With self-satisfied smiles, the Committee of 101 mistook the disappearances as proof that their gambit with military force had worked. And, with a magnanimous gesture, they allowed Smith to remain in town. Without his gang, they considered him harmless. Besides, he'd shown many acts of charity and generosity — hadn't he?

Soapy must have privately gloated at how the vanishing gang ruse had worked in his favour. The remaining lawless element in Skagway that had not previously been within his control were fearful of military justice. They immediately turned to the suave con man as their protector and leader. His old gang gradually filtered back into town as well, and by February Skagway was back to its infamous worst. And Soapy was stronger than ever before.

Chapter 8
Telegraph to Nowhere

news report distributed throughout the U.S. on February 25, 1898, confirmed Soapy's rule over Skagway. It claimed that Skagway was "beyond description," a place where robbery was just a fact of life. It reported that eight bodies were picked up on the White Pass on February 15, and that violence was only the beginning.

When 12 robberies and a murder were reported on the White Pass Trail in one day, Frank Reid and his vigilantes had had enough. They agreed in another mass meeting of miners to take action again, and this time there would not be a false show of force with soldiers. To formalize their intent, The Committee of 101 purchased space in one of the Skagway newspapers and posted a threatening message to the area's undesirables to get out of town or else.

A rebirth of this mob of do-gooders was the last thing Soapy wanted to see in the town he now controlled completely. Acting immediately, he gathered his forces, canvassed the town's influential businessmen, and pressed his acquaintances for loyalty. Something drastic had to be done to rid Skagway of this committee of 101 bad apples, he said. Within hours he had their support and Soapy posted his own handbills around Skagway.

Announcement
The business interests of Skagway propose to put a stop to the lawless acts of many newcomers. We hereby summon all good citizens to a meeting at which these matters will be discussed. Come one, come all. Immediate action will be taken for relief. Let this be a warning to those cheechakos who are disgracing our city. The meeting will be held at Sylvester Hall at 8 p.m. sharp.

Jefferson R. Smith, Chairman

The turnout to Smith's meeting was jammed to overflowing. Soapy opened the discussion with every eloquent trick he knew to fire the crowd in support of his contention that a new crop of interlopers was destroying the friendly God-fearing environment in Skagway. He pointed a finger at Reid. And with his gang members strategically placed in the crowd applauding his assertions, Soapy proposed a committee sanctioned by the entire community of Skagway. He suggested a group that could show the riffraff who was really running the town. The assembly cheered Soapy and his idea, and then happily elected him to serve in a permanent capacity as chairman of Skagway's law and order committee. This committee decided to call themselves The Committee of 303.

New signs were posted through town and up the White Pass Trail:

Public Warning
The body of men calling themselves the Committee of One Hundred and One are hereby notified that any overt act committed by them will be met promptly by the law abiding citizens of Skagway and each member and their property will be held responsible for any unlawful act committed on their part. The Law and Order Committee of Three Hundred and Three will see that justice is dealt out to its fullest extent and no Blackmailers or Vigilantes will be tolerated.

Signed; Law and Order Committee of Three Hundred and Three

This fast action by Soapy managed to divide Skagway into two camps and the officially recognized group won out. Suitably proud of his *coup d'état*, Smith had the number *317* painted above the door of Jeff Smith's Parlor, marking it as the Law and Order Committee headquarters. It also served to remind everyone in Skagway that the new committee had gathered 14 new members.

After the tussle for power, the *Skaguay News* tried to dispel the rumours of lawlessness reaching the southern cities. In a report in October 1897, Skagway was described as having grown from a collection of tents "to a fair-sized town with well-laid-out streets and numerous frame buildings, stores, saloons, gambling houses, dance houses, and a population of about 20,000." According to Customs Office records, 5000 stampeders had landed in Skagway in February 1898 alone.

It was during the hurly-burly of that tremendous spurt in growth that Superintendent Sam Steele of the NWMP arrived in Skagway. A burly, fearless lawman, Steele had helped rid the west of whisky traders. He'd policed the construction of the Canadian Pacific Railway (CPR) and had even prevented a war between Natives and white settlers in British Columbia by the force of his character. But even with all of this experience, Steele was somewhat cowed by the wild town of Skagway. Nevertheless, he was determined to keep Smith and his corruption out of Canadian territory for fear that Soapy's gang would take control if they ever got established in Dawson City. Steele made sure the NWMP were on duty at the summits of both passes, and he had machine guns installed at the ready to block any plans Soapy might have had to expand his influence into Canada.

The NWMP monitored the passing torrent of stampeders and oversaw the collection of custom duties at the top of the passes. After the first season of the gold rush, the Canadian customs officials made plans to transport $150,000 in gold and bank notes south to Victoria. Inspector Zachary T. Wood's concern about boarding a boat in Skagway with the customs revenue demonstrated the high level of fear everyone had about Soapy's town. While Sam Steele and his officers controlled the entry to the Klondike, the trail leading to the White Pass was infested with Soapy's men and the Canadian police had no authority there. Rather than risk a robbery on that route, Wood decided to try a ruse. He travelled alone, like a destitute gold seeker returning home, and made it all the way across the Chilkoot to Dyea. But Wood didn't realize Soapy's spies were everywhere. When his gang caught wind of Wood's mission, they attempted to confront the inspector at Skagway Bay and steal the government purse.

Wood, however, courageously managed to hold off his attackers at gunpoint until he reached the Skagway dock, at which point he made a wild dash down the dock toward the *Tartar*. The captain of the ship, who had been advised of Wood's planned arrival, was ready. As Wood reached the gangway with Soapy's men in noisy pursuit, a sudden fringe of sailors aiming rifles at the pursuers appeared on deck.

No robbery had actually been attempted. If it had, it might have resulted in an international incident that would have exposed Soapy's criminal grip on Skagway, saving thousands from being victimized. Sadly, that didn't happen.

Many who arrived in Skagway had never before been away from their homes. They were bewildered, tired, and incredibly naïve about their strange surroundings. The only thing they or their families back home really knew was that the journey up the coast to Skagway was a treacherous one. News of shipwrecks was regular fodder for headlines in the south. The year 1889 held the record, averaging three a month. Inexperienced pilots navigated the uncharted waters through fog that formed when wet winds were warmed by the Japanese current and then cooled upon rising over the coastal islands.

Soapy thought about the anxiety experienced by the families left behind, and he soon took advantage with a clever scam. All it required was a man who knew how to operate a telegraph key, a little paint for a sign, and a few hundred yards of wire. With much fanfare, Soapy set up the Dominion Telegraph Service by taking over one of the buildings in Skagway. The "telegraph office," furnished and manned, proudly claimed it could send and receive messages from anywhere in the world. For only five dollars for ten words, every stampeder could send home news of his safe arrival. Many newcomers, of course, wanted to do exactly that. None, however, bothered to check to see where the wire led from behind the office. If they had, they might have realized the cables were only nailed to the back wall, with the other end disappearing somewhere in the water of Skagway Bay.

Soapy Smith

The service the men got from Soapy's telegraph office was prompt, courteous, and officious. Privacy was assured to those who couldn't write and needed to dictate their messages. The telegrams were "remitted" without delay. Obligingly, the service accepted replies on a collect basis. Most were received within a few hours of a stampeder's "good news" transmission home, before he had a chance to hit the trails for the gold fields. The newcomers gladly paid the reply fee and read their loved ones' best wishes. Often the congratulations on a safe journey came with a plea of cash to answer some sort of domestic emergency. Soapy's men, of course, accepted the miners' money for transfer — not back home, but directly into Soapy's strongbox.

Soapy had other equally creative services in place, including the Information Bureau, which purported to have the latest word about the Klondike and even offered maps and weather reports. But instead of supplying useful information, the "bureau" gang members gathered every bit of detail they could from each sucker — the size of his outfit, how much cash he was carrying, the names of his friends, and his family background. These were all details they could record and use in their other phony enterprises. Of course, the richest of the suckers were always steered to the gambling den.

The gang played every angle to prey on the cheechakos' fears. Newcomers were told that maps that identified poison springs along the trails could be bought at the Merchant Exchange, which was really just another false-fronted shack.

Once the newcomers fresh off the boat were steered to the dimly lit "exchange," they were quickly relieved of their money. If a stampeder wanted his freight shipped to the top of the White Pass, Soapy's organization was happy to comply. It was usually too late when the stampeder discovered the freight line didn't really exist and his goods had been sold from under him.

Soapy's gang, in the guise of freight agents, newspaper reporters, knowledgeable old-timers, and clergymen, ringed the docks waiting for suckers to arrive. If the spies Soapy paid to ride back and forth from Seattle, San Francisco, and Vancouver to befriend the stampeders failed to report which of the newcomers had the most cash, it didn't take long for the affable gang members at the docks to make that determination. Invariably, they would either steer their victims to one of Soapy's fraudulent businesses or stake him out for a robbery on the trails.

Soapy was able to steal with total disregard for consequences. Newcomers often found themselves completely stripped of their wealth — unable to go to the Klondike without the year's worth of supplies the NWMP insisted upon at the summits of the Chilkoot or White Pass, and unable to afford passage home. When that stalemate occurred, a kindly gentleman with a pointed Mephisto-like beard sometimes appeared, and out of Christian charity advanced the broke prospector just enough money to get home. Soapy's generosity served two purposes: victims returned south with proof Skagway was not utterly bereft of kind and caring people, and Soapy got rid of complainers who might spoil future business.

With the techniques he'd used in Denver and Creede to hunt for Bill's Luck, Soapy was the closest thing Skagway had to Santa Claus. He made a great show of his generosity to help balance the rising tide of animosity toward him that was spreading from one end of the Lynn Canal to the other. Should a gold seeker with a wife fall victim to his gang, Soapy would graciously comfort her with partial monetary restitution to keep her from grumbling too loudly. He also paid for her passage back to civilization. Soapy maintained accounts at merchants' stores to provide provisions and fuel to the needy. He paid the funeral expenses for dead miners no one claimed. He was always the first to drop money into the donation plate at the Union Church, always the first to pass his black hat when contributions to a widow's relief fund were necessary, and always the first to come up with ways to pluck the heartstrings of the homesick miners. His largesse even extended to dogs.

Every mode of transportation was considered by the stampeders who were planning their trek to the goldfields. Often that included sled dogs that the newcomers had bought for outrageously inflated prices in Seattle. Unfortunately, every size and breed met the stampeders' loose definition of sled dog. Most could not be trained to pull a sled and were abandoned in Skagway to forage for themselves in packs.

Skagway was overrun with the curs. Soapy, of course, had a solution. It was an Adopt-A-Dog campaign and he started it by claiming six strays of his own.

With a tremble in his voice he pleaded with the passing hordes to think of God's creatures and contribute to a relief fund dedicated to feeding the poor critters. Many stampeders, who couldn't afford to feed a mongrel of their own, were so touched by Soapy that they added to the fund's coffers anyway. The con man did feed the strays, but only enough to keep them alive and friendly long enough to be sold as pack animals to other stampeders who didn't know any better.

Chapter 9
Soapy Milks the Military

Moving the men out of Skagway to the Klondike had become a problem of logistics to the merchants in town. The idea for a railroad from Skagway saw its genesis at a meeting of two men, one with the money and the other with the skills: Sir Thomas Tancrede (representative of the British financiers, the Close Brothers), and Michael J. "The Irish Prince" Heney, a man who'd helped build the Canadian Pacific Railway. Both men had arrived in Skagway with the same purpose in mind. Tancrede had travelled north with Samuel H. Graves of Chicago and E.C. Hawkins of Seattle, surveyed the mountains, and concluded that a railroad would be impossible. Heney, however, had no qualms. After an evening together in the St. James Hotel bar, he got Tancrede to agree he was right.

In April 1898, the White Pass & Yukon Railroad Company (WP&YR) was incorporated.

When the railway surveyors arrived in Skagway on May 27, 1898, they found a townsite in the possession of squatters. Title to land was hotly disputed and men with no rights were still demanding payment for right-of-way from the ocean across the gravel tidal flats to the White Pass Trail. Five preliminary surveys were made by the railway before the best available line route to the summit was determined. The mountainsides along the way were precipitous granite cliffs and thickly wooded to the timberline. Finally, a route made up of parts of each of the surveys was settled upon and the construction began. The work was difficult and dangerous. Workers, who were suspended from ropes over cliffs, blasted through solid granite. They contended with brutally cold temperatures and constant winds that tore down on them from the mountain summits. Gravel for the roadbed had to be hauled from Skagway. Nearly insurmountable physical hurdles had to be overcome every mile of the way. At Dead Horse Gulch, workers had to build a steel cantilever bridge (254 metres long and 81 metres high) over the canyon. At the time it was the largest bridge of its kind in the world.

Thousands of workers were needed for the construction, which presented a human hurdle to the railway. It was nearly impossible for the builders to hold their workers on the job for low wages when the goldfields were constantly calling. Consequently, the number of workers varied almost daily, with wild swings from 2000 on August 8 to just 700 only days later when news reached the camps that gold had been discovered in Atlin. The railway didn't get back to full crew strength until October when enough new stampeders arrived in Skagway. The men were paid a paltry three dollars a day for their sacrifices. But for those who were robbed by Soapy's men before even setting out, or for those who had given up their quest, it was the only work to be had.

The railway also had to contend with Soapy and his gang. Long before the construction had begun, Soapy had organized his gang along the White Pass Trail. They posed as old sourdoughs who offered fellow stampeders advice, as well as a warm fire and a friendly welcome. Robbery, of course, was always their motive.

In an attempt to hold off Soapy, the railroad used an effective threat. Michael Heney was usually able to enforce an edict of "no liquor in camp." Soapy's gang members were warned to stay away. But when construction work started at Rocky Point on the line, one of Soapy's men arrived and set up a gambling and drinking tent. Heney ordered the man to leave but the ruffian refused. Heney stared him down and then called for the camp foreman, Mike Foy. Soapy's man reached for his rifle expecting a roust, but Heney pointed upward to a big rock looming above the tent. "That rock has to be out of there by five tomorrow morning, not a minute later," he commanded Foy. The Skagway Terror's minion scoffed, calling Heney's bluff, and went to bed laughing.

The next morning Foy sent some of his men scrambling up the mountain to put dynamite around the rock and then had one of his crew wake up the barkeep. When the man still refused to move, Foy went to the tent himself. "In one minute, I'm giving the order to touch off the fuse. It will then burn for one minute and that rock will arrive here or hereabouts."

"Aw, go to hell," the ruffian replied.

"Fire!" Foy shouted to his crew and ran for cover.

He was joined by the barkeep (dressed only in his long-johns) seconds later as the dynamite exploded. The rock came crashing down over the tent and the barkeep's store of liquor in a storm of dust and debris. It appears Soapy got the message because he never again sent a gang member up the White Pass Trail to prey upon the railway crew.

On August 25, after two months of backbreaking labour, the White Pass & Yukon Railroad had a passenger train running for 22 kilometres. Track reached the White Pass summit, 873 metres above sea level on February 18, 1899. By then, the railroad found it had to deal with still another human problem. The precise location of the Canadian-American border was still in dispute. Canada continued to claim the border should be Skagway, while the Americans contended it should be beyond the White Pass summit at Log Cabin. It took an international mediator to settle the border argument as the White Pass option. But when the railroad reached that location they were told by the NWMP that the workers could not cross into Canada.

An inventive American named "Stikine" Bill Robinson took the matter in hand his own way. Robinson was the general manager of the Red Line Transportation Company, a firm set up by the WP&YR. When the railway was completed only as far as the White Pass summit, the Red Line contracted to "fill the gap" by freighting supplies between the end of the rail and Lake Bennett. According to the railway's president, Samuel Graves, Stikine Bill had "a considerable reputation as a taskmaster whose bulk and mastery of profanity could provoke the indolent into spirited action." It seems Stikine Bill had also taken a leaf or two from Soapy's book of tactics. With a case of scotch and a box of cigars presented to the NWMP's lone guard as a personal gift, Robinson proceeded to drink the constable under the table. When the guard finally awoke from his drunken stupor two days after his friendly party with the husky railwayman, he saw that construction had continued unchecked to the shores of Summit Lake, a few kilometres down the White Pass Trail into Canadian territory. At that point, for the railway at least, there was no turning back.

By the way the railroad was pushed through, it was obvious the Americans gave little thought to Canada's sovereignty, even though patriotism was on every American's mind for another reason at the time. The sinking of the U.S. battleship *Maine* in Havana harbour on February 15, 1898, with the loss of 260 of her crew, had brought a sudden flush of patriotic fervour to the American miners in Skagway. Many were already broke or discouraged by their failure in the gold-fields and were looking for an affordable way to get home. The Spanish–American War seemed a fortuitous answer. And it presented another chance for a last trim of their fortunes by Soapy.

The con man may not have been directly involved, but it's certain that at least three members of his gang played a role in a final fleecing of miners who were determined to join the fighting in the war. Responding to a hand-painted sign that was hung over the doorway to a tent proclaiming it was the U.S. Army Recruiting Center, the hope-drained (or patriotic) men in Skagway lined up. Inside they were met with a curt official who welcomed them and thanked them for remembering the *Maine*. Once a man had been asked a few cursory questions such as his name and date of birth, he was ushered into the rear of the tent by the army "chaplain" and told to strip off his clothes so an army "doctor" could give him the necessary physical examination.

While the doctor performed his fake exam, the chaplain searched the recruit's clothes and outfit, pilfering anything of value that the hapless miner still had. If the ruse was discovered, the victim usually ended up bodily tossed from the rear of the tent in his underwear, or with an armload of his least desirable clothes, and a threat to keep quiet or face a gun barrel.

Publicly, however, Soapy took a much different position. By the spring of 1898, he was obviously basking in the glow of his power. He appeared to enjoy the adulation of Skagway's general population as a "defender of law and justice." He fed that popularity further with gregarious shows of charity by way of donations of all sorts to the less fortunate, paid from his ill-gotten gains. He was proud to hold sway in any gathering as the man who ran Skagway. Soapy made a point of staying informed about world events and politics. He avidly followed news reports that made their way to Skagway from civilization in Seattle and San Francisco when the steamers that disgorged his steady flow of victims arrived with newspapers.

Soapy may have read in a newspaper that under the authorization of the Volunteer Bill of April 23, 1898, U.S. President William McKinley wanted citizens to provide manpower for the First Volunteer Cavalry Regiment, the "Rough Riders." McKinley called for 125,000 volunteers from the seven western states and territories. The figure soon rose to 267,000. Three regiments were to be formed in the west: the first in the four territories, which included Alaska, the second in Wyoming, and the third in the Dakotas.

After President McKinley's call to arms, Soapy may have also read that Senator Frances E. Warren of Wyoming had introduced a bill in the U.S. Congress authorizing federal funds for those volunteer units. These funds were put under the control of the unit organizers. After the Wyoming unit was formed on March 8, 1898, for example, the U.S. secretary of war, Russell A. Lager, allocated $250,000 for organizational expenses, $197,000 for transportation and horses, $31,392 for equipment, and $15,000 for subsistence. Soapy may have thought he'd discovered a gold mine of a different kind ... in Washington, D.C.

That considered, it was predictable that Soapy would announce he was going to form a militia group in support of Teddy Roosevelt's Rough Riders. Volunteers whom Smith attracted were not limited to the victimized miners who entered the phony recruiting tent. In fact, Soapy made a point of calling his recruiting station the only "official" recruiting centre in Skagway, to pre-empt anyone else from getting the same idea. If Soapy did devise the scam to drive volunteers his way to the "honest" station, it was an ingenious ploy.

As soon as men began to sign up, the unit was named Company A, First Regiment of the National Guard of Alaska. Soapy was elected captain. One of Skagway's better Three-Card Monte dealers, John Foley, was named first lieutenant. The bouncer at Clancy's, J.T. Millar, became the first sergeant. And the bartender at the Klondike Saloon was picked as the unit's chaplain. Smith did what he could to make the unit as real as possible without the advantage of uniforms. He bought all the silk ribbon in town and had badges made for each of the recruits. When there were more men than ribbons, Soapy had the badges sketched on butcher paper. It didn't seem to matter to the men. Wearing ribbon or paper, they were all treated as equal members in the National Guard of Alaska, and they wore their badges with pride.

Soapy Smith

Once Soapy commanded this legally recognized force of recruits, he gave the perpetrators of the fake recruiting station a public scourging. He demanded that the trio (all known members of his gang) return everything they'd stolen, and warned them that "swift military justice" would be served on them if they tried it again.

Soapy then took his command up an even more serious path. He began drilling his recruits on Broadway Avenue. By Sunday, May 1, 1898, when they had managed a reasonable facsimile of lock-step marching, Soapy paraded them for all the citizens to see. The men marched from the waterfront with their captain leading the way on horseback. Soapy had strong-armed all the saloon musicians in Skagway to march with the volunteers as a band to add a festive flavour to the event. But, in spite of the drill training the men were given, Soapy's command showed a few holes. When the parade reached 5th Street and Broadway, Captain Smith turned the lead unit to the right but the rest of the contingent went left. It took two blocks of stepping at a quick march for him to regain his place at the head of the parade. And when Soapy passed by the Princess Hotel he encountered another obstacle that stopped his marchers in their tracks. When Babe Davenport, the most famous madam in town, heard the band she hurriedly gathered her girls into the street in various states of undress and demanded that Skagway's patriotic captain form a Women's Auxiliary. "You're next," Soapy replied courteously, reeling his men around the impasse.

Soapy Milks the Military

Soapy Smith, mounted on a white horse, prepares to lead the
Independence Day parade. Skagway, Alaska, July 4, 1898.

He marched them for several more circuits of the town.
After an hour and a half, he stopped the parade amid a crowd
of well-wishers at the city hall. There, the crowd called for a
speech. Soapy climbed off his horse and mounted a newly
constructed review stand. "There is one man who, in this
terrible strife, has transcended the bounds of fair war. He has
murdered the helpless and the weak, debauched women,
butchered and starved little children." Soapy, ever the drama

director, called for an effigy of General Valeriano Weyler of Cuba, and it was put to the torch.

Soapy then offered a passionate address to his cheering militia. "You are fine brave men, each and every one of you," he proclaimed, "and I am sure that you will unhesitatingly follow me anywhere and at any time." The crowd applauded as he led the majority of his thirsty troops down the street to his saloon, where barkeepers were ready to push the booze across the board. In an hour Soapy sold more than $2500 in alcohol, proving his men would follow him, at least so long as he had a bottle.

Though Soapy had legitimately gathered the recruits for the National Guard of Alaska, when he offered their service to the secretary of war in Washington, he received a polite refusal. However, it came with compliments about the con man's patriotism. The refusal was disappointing but Soapy displayed the letter on the wall of his gambling parlor with pride just the same.

Soapy reprised the display of military power on July 4, 1898. American Independence Day was celebrated with all the pomp and gaiety that the Skagway residents could muster. The streets were lined with red, white, and blue bunting. American flags festooned most businesses and everyone in town was in a party mood. Firecrackers popped, six-guns cracked, and even dynamite boomed as the people of Skagway waited restlessly for the parade to begin down

Broadway Avenue. When it did, it was a moment that clearly defined just how powerful the pale-skinned con man in the black suit had become in Skagway.

Sitting astride his prancing dapple-grey horse, Captain Jefferson Smith proudly waved a white sombrero as he passed. Children were showered with candy, liberally tossed into the air by Soapy's trailing line of ladies. His private militia, the Skagway "Guards," marched in perfect cadence behind them as a brass band blared. The entire town followed to a decorated stage where none other than the governor of Alaska wholeheartedly greeted Soapy.

Chapter 10
One "Poke" Too Many

Soapy's men may have thought John D. Stewart was a bumpkin. He wore a hat one size smaller than his head, ragged high-waisted trousers, and a dull vacant look that testified he'd spent too many months searching for gold in the bush around Atlin. But the gang members also recognized Stewart as a grade A mark by the buckskin bag of nuggets he was toting. Stewart was among the first of the successful miners due to make their way from Dawson City to Skagway and points south to spend their gold.

There are various stories of how Stewart was separated from his poke, but the accepted version seems to best fit the way Soapy's gang operated. Although Skagway's reputation as a thieves' paradise was known to everyone in Alaska, by the time Stewart decided to head home to Nanaimo, British Columbia, he couldn't keep himself from proudly gushing about his success as he made his way down the White Pass Trail. He showed off his $2700 in gold to anyone who would stop and listen. When he arrived in Skagway on July 7, Stewart had been warned several times that carrying 12 pounds of gold was asking for a robbery. Friends advised him to avoid Soapy Smith's men and to deposit the gold in a hotel safe until he had booked passage home. On July 8, however, Stewart met two saintly advisors — Old Man Triplett and Reverend Bowers.

The two elderly men were posing as gold buyers who had recently come to Skagway on behalf of a large assaying company "below," and they convinced Stewart he could get a better price for his gold at Jeff Smith's Parlor than he could when he reached Victoria. Stewart accompanied Bowers and Triplett to the rear of Soapy's saloon on Holly Street where a price was to be negotiated. In the midst of that discussion another gang member, who was dressed like a Klondiker, scooped up the poke with a loud laugh as if making a joke. Once he had it, though, he ran for the door. Stewart made to grab the thief in the bar but other gang members played at misunderstanding what was going on and they jostled Stewart as if he were a drunk. Stewart, confused and angry, began shouting for help. By the time the miner reached the doorway, of course, his laughing thief had disappeared.

When he realized he'd been taken, Stewart went to U.S.

Deputy Marshal Taylor and detailed his loss, but with little success — Taylor was on Soapy's payroll. Taylor asked the distraught miner if he could identify the culprit, but Stewart said he could not. With regret, Taylor suggested Stewart head back to the Klondike and just dig out another $2700-worth of gold. The miner was flabbergasted by the lawman's attitude. Playing the "big man," Stewart had ordered goods from Skagway merchants that he planned to take back to Nanaimo, but without his poke he had to cancel his purchases. This meant that the businessmen in Skagway also felt the sting of this robbery. When Charles deWitt, owner of one of the larger packing outfits heard what happened, he too began complaining about the robbery. DeWitt didn't care so much about Stewart's money, but he did care about what the theft could mean to business in Skagway that spring.

The successful miners could make their way to the ocean by travelling downriver from Dawson City to St. Michael. From there they could board steamers headed south. It was a longer route but one deWitt feared the miners might take if word reached them that the first man to come out through Skagway with gold had been robbed. DeWitt said action was necessary. He took Stewart to Frank Reid's friend, Captain Sperry, immediately. By noon, Captain Sperry, Frank Reid, and Major Tanner had roused the Committee of 101.

Stewart's robbery was being recounted all over town by knots of angry men. DeWitt's fear that rich prospectors would turn away from Skagway became a rumour that spread amongst the citizens like a flash flood. Within an hour it seemed to have become a reality. The men were outraged that Soapy Smith's greed had destroyed them all financially.

Soapy's spies were running reports of unrest from every side of town. One informant told him that an outfitter named M.K. Kalem was urging a crowd to resort to violence only a few blocks away. Soapy pulled on a mackinaw, thrust a revolver into each pocket, and charged to the impromptu rally. Though he didn't expose his guns, it was clear he held them in his pockets and was ready to fire as he pushed to the front of the mob. "You're a lot of cowardly rope-pulling sons of bitches!" Smith taunted the crowd to act, but out of fear of bloodshed the men dispersed.

The Committee of 101 had been inactive after Soapy's sneaky town meeting that had put him in permanent charge of the Committee of 317. But Reid had learned his lesson. Instead of leading the most vocal objectors like a lynch mob, Reid asked what passed for a chamber of commerce in Skagway to consider the matter of the theft and what should be done about it. Seventeen of the merchants gathered and they elected a chairman. Samuel Graves, president of the White Pass & Yukon Railroad, took the lead and promptly adjourned the meeting so that Judge Charles A. Sehlbrede could be called in from Dyea. Graves convinced his committee to wait until 11:00 p.m. before reviewing the matter again. When the judge arrived from Dyea, he and a small group of vigilantes called on Smith. Soapy met them with disdain.

Stewart, he claimed, had lost the gold gambling, but Soapy said he was willing to consider returning it anyway. Sehlbrede gave Smith a deadline of 4:00 p.m. to do just that.

Perhaps it was issuance of that deadline that changed Soapy's mind about co-operating. He already saw his authority undermined by the vigilantes. With Judge Sehlbrede in their camp, they seemed to have the power of the law on their side as well. His own men, including Old Man Triplett, were counselling him to back down and put an end to the matter before it got out of hand. It was only $2700 after all, and a thousand times that in nuggets and gold dust would be hauled down the White Pass Trail and into their laps within a few weeks. But the insult of the ultimatum, and the fact that his own men were advising retreat from the vigilantes, might have made Smith stubborn. He flatly refused to co-operate and threatened to cut off the ears of any man who tried to return the gold.

As the clock ticked closer to the four o'clock deadline, a mood of dread fell over Skagway and a quiet crowd began to gather outside Jeff Smith's Parlor. A newspaper reporter warned Soapy there would be serious trouble if the gold was not returned. But the con man, who'd been drinking for several hours, shouted loud enough for the crowd outside to hear. "By God, trouble is what I'm looking for!" Soapy moved to the door with a rifle and faced the crowd with a sneer. He shouted that he had 500 men ready to do his bidding if anyone was brave enough to force the issue. The crowd's murmur died to silence but the miners stared back defiantly. This time they would not back down in facing the Skagway Terror. Eye-to-eye, Soapy challenged the mute men and when they didn't move away, he returned to the bar grumbling about ingrates.

Just four days earlier he'd been the town hero. He'd sat with the governor and led the Fourth of July parade to the cheers of thousands. What the devil was happening? How had all that adoration turned to hatred so quickly? Soapy was confused and seething.

The deadline passed and Smith remained inside his parlor drinking whisky. Offices and shops were quietly closed. Saloons locked their doors. The biggest cowards in Soapy's gang slipped away and headed to the forest and its mountain trails. From the docks, the echo of spirited speeches floated to Broadway Avenue on the breeze from Skagway Bay. Citizens flocked to Sperry's warehouse to discuss what the next step of action should be. Soapy sent some of his gang members to the warehouse to monitor the vigilantes' planning. The con man had decided to bluff his way out of this trouble with threats of reprisal, as he'd successfully done before, but he wanted to know what to expect.

He continued pouring himself whisky. Between drinks, while the citizens' meeting took place, Soapy paced the street with his rifle. When he came across anyone, he hurled insults. In his state of mind he was fast becoming a danger to everyone, including his own gang.

The vigilante meeting descended into chaos. Soapy's

men managed to disrupt and provoke, bringing discussion to an impasse. But the sentiment of the core group of vigilantes was clear. Waiting another five hours until the official 11:00 p.m. meeting of the Merchants' Committee seemed pointless. Soapy wasn't going to comply. Action had to be taken immediately before he had a chance to defuse the emotion of the town.

With a campaign of whispers, the vigilantes spread the word that they would gather again at 8:00 p.m. This time they would meet at the Sylvester Hall on the docks. No one bothered to notify their chairman, Samuel Graves. Perhaps the vigilantes considered him an impediment to swift justice, or perhaps it was because Graves was a relative newcomer to Skagway. He hadn't been involved with the original Committee of 101 vigilantes, the same men who had jumped Captain Moore's claim in the earliest days of the settlement.

The citizenry began to gather early and by nine o'clock the number of dissenters had grown so large that, after electing Thomas Whitten of the Golden Graves Hotel as their new chairman, the crowd decided to reconvene in a larger space. Whitten knew they needed a location where Soapy's influence could be restricted, so he moved the meeting to the far end of the Juneau dock, out of earshot to the shore. To make sure their discussion could not be reported, Whitten also posted guards and had a chain draped across the entrance to the dock. Frank Reid, Jesse Murphy, J.M. Tanner, and a man named Landers were assigned guard duty. Reid was the only man armed. He had borrowed a Colt revolver from a friend earlier in the day after Soapy threatened to settle matters with him personally.

Soapy's spies alerted the agitated half-drunk crime boss about the second meeting shortly before nine o'clock. Billy Saportas, a newspaperman on Soapy's payroll, had been covering the meetings. Saportas dashed off a quick note to Soapy, urging him to act. "The crowd is angry. If you want to do anything, do it quick." Fearfully, several cronies again advised him to take the bitter pill and return Stewart's gold, but Soapy adamantly refused. "I'll drive the bastards into the bay!" he vowed.

Soapy braced for a fight. He slipped a tiny derringer into his sleeve, grabbed his Winchester .30/30 rifle from the bar, slung it over his shoulder, and steamed out of his parlor. There was an angry glare in his grey eyes as he clomped down the wooden sidewalk on Holly Street, muttering how he was going to "teach these damn sons of bitches a lesson!" He had drawn a crowd of his own by the time he reached State Street, a road that ran parallel to Broadway and ended at the docks. "Chase yourselves home to bed!" he shouted at his entourage, waving the Winchester. The crowd backed up a respectful distance but no one completely retreated. This was just too exciting a moment in Skagway history to be missed. Soapy cursed at them and moved on in frustration. By this time about a dozen of his gang were also sidling along a short distance behind him.

Soapy Smith

Turning onto Broadway, Soapy encountered his partner, saloonkeeper John Clancy, and Clancy's wife, who were taking a late evening stroll with their six-year-old son. Clancy warned Soapy that the mob on the dock would not be cowed by one man waving a rifle. "Turn around and get the gold from your safe," Clancy implored, holding on to Soapy's shoulder.

"Johnny, you better leave me alone." Soapy pulled a revolver from his pocket and prodded Clancy's side.

"All right." Clancy shook his head and backed away from his partner's boozy breath. "If you want to get killed, go ahead." As they made room for Soapy to pass, Clancy's wife burst into tears.

The dock he was steaming towards had been erected on a causeway of gravel that stretched out into the bay over the muddy tidal flats. When Soapy reeled to the dock he could see the clutch of vigilantes milling at the far end of the wooden structure, and at the entrance to the dock he ran right into Frank Reid. Reid told him he wasn't welcome.

"I should have got rid of you three months ago!" Soapy barked. In a show of drunken bluster, he waved his Winchester and demanded to know what Reid was doing there. "Let me by!" he ordered. He waved the rifle towards the end of the wharf and made a bluff to strike Reid in the head with the barrel.

Defending himself with his left hand, Reid grabbed the rifle. Soapy tried to tug it away, but Reid had a solid hold and pulled the barrel down towards his groin. At the same time he reached for his Colt with his right hand.

"For God's sake, don't shoot!" Soapy roared in panic — but simultaneously, both men did. Reid's hammer clicked but his six-gun didn't fire. Soapy pulled the trigger on his rifle and a bullet tore through Reid's groin, shattering the lower part of his right hip. Reid already had his revolver pointed and he fired again. A bullet ripped through Soapy's heart, killing him almost instantly. As Soapy fell, he managed to fire his rifle a second time, blasting Reid in the leg. Reid returned fire again, shooting the con man in the leg above his left knee.

It was a spontaneous moment of mayhem. Seconds before, neither man had had the intent to kill. In an instant, however, Soapy's reign as the Terror of Skagway ended in a puff of gun smoke. Murphy scuttled forward to get Soapy's rifle, and he held off the gang members who had their own guns drawn. The echo of the shots threw a blanket of silence over the bay for a few moments as the crowd on the beach and the wharf tried to make sense of what had happened. When Soapy's gang saw the vigilantes running towards them along the dock, they scattered. As the crowd reached the fallen men, Frank Reid raised himself on one arm. "I'm badly hurt but I got him first," he said. Cheers echoed from mountain to mountain.

On a cot taken from a nearby cabin, Reid was carried to the Bishop Rowe Hospital. The knot of miners surrounding him hailed their hero as he repeated, "I got the sonofabitch! ... I got the sonofabitch!"

Dr. F.B. Whiting, a White Pass & Yukon Railroad surgeon, met the men at Reid's cabin office and hastily examined his wounds. Everyone's attention was focused on Reid, their hero of the moment. Soapy's body lay ignored at the dock in a blood-seeping heap. Judge Sehlbrede, fearing immediate retaliation by Soapy's gang, quickly swore Si Tanner in as deputy marshal. With a rifle he borrowed from Billy Moore, Tanner quickly deputized 25 of the vigilantes and ordered them to guard the docks and spread out in search of gang members. He urged everyone in town to arm themselves for their protection. Si Tanner then shut the town down. He clapped an embargo on every vessel in the harbour until all of Soapy's followers had been rounded up. The day after the shooting, all the saloons in town remained closed. What had been a wild noisy town only a few hours earlier had become a hushed battlefield, with everyone from the meekest merchant to the biggest miner on guard for a gang attack.

With no other place to run, most of the gang scattered into the bush along the White Pass Trail, Reverend Bowers, Old Man Triplett, and Slim Jim Foster among them. After hiding there for two nights, Triplett caved in. "I'm going to get something to eat," he said. "I'd rather be hung on a full stomach than die of starvation in these goddamn mountains." The old man took the trail back to Skagway as if nothing had changed in his life. He walked straight to a restaurant and calmly ordered himself a meal. The vigilantes moved in to take him into custody, but Triplett managed to convince his captors to allow him to eat the meal he'd ordered first.

When the word spread that the nefarious gang member was inside dining as if nothing had changed, an angry crowd of miners who'd been tensely preparing for a gunfight gathered on the street. Though he was uncertain whether a rope was waiting for him or not, Triplett relaxed and ate his meal. When he was done, the vigilantes walked him to the city hall and locked him up. That afternoon Bowers and Foster were spotted and quickly seized as well.

Soapy's body had been lying unattended throughout most of the night of the shooting. Many miners felt it should simply be dragged to the end of the wharf and dumped into the sea. But, eventually, the body was taken to the doctor's surgery where Soapy's cause of death was officially determined and death portraits were taken. On July 11, three days after he was killed, his corpse had to be disposed of but both the Baptist and the Methodist ministers refused to officiate at his funeral. Reverend Sinclair, a Presbyterian, finally came forward.

The services were organized with Soapy's body put on public view, more as proof that the Skagway Terror was truly dead than out of respect. While the citizens of the town were willing to allow Soapy a burial rather than an unholy dump in the bay, they would not allow his remains to rest in consecrated ground. His pine coffin was carried to the outskirts of the cemetery in an express wagon, preceded by a hack that held Mr. Butler, a prominent member of the Committee of

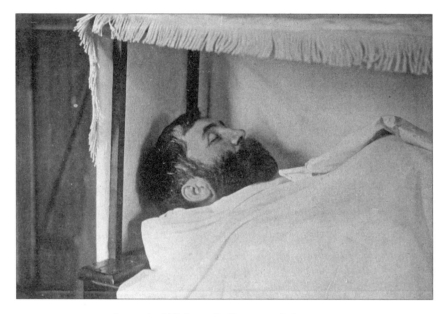

Soapy Smith's funeral. Skagway, Alaska, 1898.

101, three lawyers who'd worked for Smith, and the minister. Reverend Sinclair read part of the text from Proverbs 13:15 to the handful of attendants a couple of metres outside the cemetery. "Good understanding giveth favour: but the way of transgressors is hard," Sinclair muttered, putting an end to Soapy's interment as fast as the con man's hands had once moved with his walnut shells. A wooden board was all that marked his grave, with the following etched inscription: *Jefferson R. Smith. Died July 8, 1898. Age 38 years.*

By Sunday night, Reid's wounds were proving to be serious. The Winchester bullet that entered his body five centimetres above his groin on the right had made its exit in his back beside his spine. Passing through him, it had fractured his pelvic bone. Despite prompt treatment in the few days following his gunfight, Reid's wound was starting to turn septic.

Frank Reid's sacrifice was on the mind of everyone in Skagway. The milling crowd, having tired of hunting for gang members, wanted revenge. "Hang them! Hang the whole gang!" they screamed outside the city hall, swinging ropes. "Bring out Triplett! This is just right for his neck!"

Si Tanner did his best to calm the vigilantes. He faced them and shouted back, "Don't hang the evidence! Let law and order rule and we'll get Stewart his money back. We have a lot of men inside who had nothing to do with the robbery. If you want to hang someone, hang me!" The lynch mob relaxed, but the impromptu deputy marshal wasn't taking any chances. He decided to move the gang ringleaders to the hardware store across the street, Triplett and Foster among them.

Triplett was cool and collected. But Foster was obviously in a state of near panic at the prospect of a lynching. The old man delighted in teasing Foster, describing the gruesome details of hangings he had witnessed as Foster paced the floor of the second-storey room where they'd been moved. Foster's fears finally got the best of him. At a run, he dove through the window down to French Alley. A guard in the alley tried to shoot the escaping outlaw and missed, but the gunshot brought the lynch mob running from the front of the building. When they saw Foster, they attacked with their rope. A tussle ensued with the mob leaders slipping the noose on Foster and Tanner's men removing it. This was repeated several times.

Infantry from Dyea had been summoned after the shooting. And, as luck would have it, they arrived in Skagway at precisely that moment to declare martial law. Foster was hustled back to his jail cell with only bruises and rope burns.

That night, the search for Stewart's gold ended when the poke was discovered in Soapy's trunk with $500 of it missing. The next day, 11 of Soapy's gang members were transferred to Sitka where they were charged with extortion and grand larceny. They received sentences that ranged from one to ten years. Nine others were loaded on a steamer bound for Seattle, where the police met them and arrested those who had charges pending for other crimes.

Skagway physicians operated on Frank Reid at five o'clock on Tuesday morning. He lingered for several days but on July 20, 12 days after the shooting, he finally succumbed. Attired in a new suit, Frank Reid lay in state in a flag-draped coffin at the Union Church, the one that Soapy had helped to build with his liberal donations. Skagway's first public funeral and the largest in its history followed on July 22. Reverend Wooden conducted the services, reading the Episcopal Church's ritual for the dead. Reverend Sinclair gave a long eloquent tribute to the memory of the man Skagway considered its greatest hero.

One "Poke" Too Many

Jefferson Randolph "Soapy" Smith, whose estate amounted to only $250 after all his thieving, had a grave marked with a pauper's wooden cross. Frank Reid's grave was marked with a large marble stone, erected by the community, with the inscription: *He gave his life for the honour of Skagway.*

Not far from Frank Reid's resting place, the grave of a local prostitute bears a similar inscription — *She gave her honour for the life of Skagway.* This humorous twist on the quirky meaning of community and of human nature was typical of the men and women who found their way north to the Klondike.

Epilogue

Soapy Smith was an outstanding individual, if you can apply that rating to the performance of a criminal. His inventive scams to steal from the naïve and unsuspecting were so brazen that some of his gang's terms found their way into the lexicon of everyday life in America. For example, a *mark* and a *sure thing.* But Jefferson Randolph Smith was also vile and heartless. His was a life of easy money and violence. The Terror of Skagway twisted dreams and emptied wallets without regard to who or how. That greed finally did him in. Soapy revelled in his power, making up his own rules as he went along.

Standing over Soapy's grave, the reluctant minister who buried him said succinctly, "The way of transgressors is hard." If Soapy had been alive he may have added "to quit." He was addicted to the power he wielded as a crime boss. He seemed to have craved the respect and deference it gave him. But, after so many years creating false hope, Soapy ended up falling for his own con. He mistook the fear of his victims for respect.

When he died, Soapy Smith was reviled by everyone he'd preyed upon. He was buried in a pauper's grave with no more than a weather-bleached board to mark his final resting place, just a metre or two from consecrated ground.

Epilogue

Time has gained him a grudging respect, though. While the residents of Skagway called Reid a hero, it's Soapy's grave tourists still come to see and his amazing story they want to hear.

Further Reading

Becker, Ethel Anderson. *Klondike '98: E.A. Hegg's Gold Rush Album*. Portland, Oregon: Binfords & Mort., 1972.

Berton, Pierre. *City of Gold*. Toronto, Ontario: McClelland & Stewart Inc., 1992.

Berton, Pierre. *Klondike: The Last Great Gold Rush 1898–1899*. Toronto, Ontario: McClelland & Stewart Limited, 1972.

Berton, Pierre. *The Klondike Fever: The Life and Death of the Last Great Gold Rush*. New York, NY: Carroll & Graff Publishers, 1985.

Berton, Pierre. *Trails of '98*. Toronto, Ontario: McClelland & Stewart Inc., 1992.

Brennan, Ann T. *The Real Klondike Kate*. Fredericton, New Brunswick: Goose Lane Editions, 1990.

Clifford, Howard. *The Skagway Story*. Anchorage, Alaska: Alaska Northwest Publishing Company, 1975.

Cohen, Stan. *The streets were paved with gold: A pictorial history of the Klondike Gold Rush 1896–1899.* Missoula, Montana: Pictorial Histories Publishing Co., 1977.

Cooper, Michael. *Klondike Fever: The Famous Gold Rush of 1898.* New York, NY: Clarion Books, 1989.

Johnson, James Albert. *Carmack of the Klondike.* Seattle, Washington: Epicenter Press, 1990.

Morgan, Murray. *One Man's Gold Rush: A Klondike Album.* Vancouver, British Columbia: J.J. Douglas Ltd., 1967.

Robertson, Frank G. and Harris, Beth Kay. *Soapy Smith, King of the Frontier Con Men.* New York, NY: Hastings House Publishers, 1961.

About the Author

Stan Sauerwein lives and writes in Westbank, British Columbia. A freelance writer for two decades, Stan has written articles that have appeared in a variety of Canadian and U.S. magazines and newspapers. Specializing in business subjects, he has written for both corporations and governments. He is the author of seven other books — *Rattenbury: The Life and Tragic End of BC's Greatest Architect, Ma Murray: The Story of Canada's Crusty Queen of Publishing, Klondike Joe Boyle: Heroic Adventures from Gold Fields to Battlefields, Moe Norman: The Canadian Golfing Legend with the Perfect Swing, Pierre Elliott Trudeau: The Fascinating Life of Canada's Most Flamboyant Prime Minister, Lucy Maud Montgomery: The Incredible Life of the Creator of Anne of Green Gables,* and *Fintry: Lives, Loves and Dreams.*

Acknowledgements

The author would like to acknowledge the yarns Pierre Berton gifted to us all. The library of Klondike history he recorded is priceless.

Photo Credits

Cover: Alaska State Library / 277-1-9; The Denver Public Library Western History / Genealogy Department: pages 40 (Z-8903), 87 (Z-8905), 128 (Z-8904); Library and Archives Canada: page 113 (C-052213).

Amazing Author
Question and Answer

What was your inspiration for writing about Soapy Smith?

I'd been doing some research about Leadville, Colorado, for another book and Jeff Smith kept popping up. He was billed as an evil, heartless mobster and perhaps the frontier West's first gang leader. He'd managed to fool P.T. Barnum with one of his scams. That's all it took. I had to know more.

What surprised you most while you were researching Smith's life?

The gullibility of the public in the mid-1800s astounded me. How anyone could fall for Smith's obvious soap con — the con that bankrolled him for everything else — quite surprised me.

What do you most admire about Soapy Smith?

There's not much, but I do admire his skills at planning and his creativity. I can't help but think that if he'd focused on legitimate business — even though I suspect he'd have no ethics there either — there's no telling where it would have taken him.

Which of Smith's escapades do you most identify with?

The Gold Brick Game, which wasn't one of Smith's inventions, captured my imagination. How a little paint, some acting, and a wild story could fool even the most wily business tycoon, showed just how attuned these cons were to the base nature of their victims. The quick transformation from office to boudoir would make a good movie scene.

What difficulties did you run into while conducting your research?

There wasn't as much written history about Smith's private life as I would have liked to include. Also the fact that many of his hijinks had become almost mythic. It was tough to get to the original story.

What part of the writing process did you enjoy most?

The research. I love research because everything and anything is worthy when I'm on the hunt. The day I have to sit down and sift it all is what I dislike the most.

What is your next project?
A book about North America's response to terrorism.

Who are your Canadian heroes?
Thanks to Altitude I've had the chance to write about some of them. Among the others: are George Mercer Dawson, Lester Pearson, Robertson Davies, Captain Bob Bartlett.

by the same author

AMAZING STORIES™

KLONDIKE JOE BOYLE

Heroic Adventures From
Gold Fields to Battlefields

HISTORY/BIOGRAPHY
by Stan Sauerwein

ISBN 1-55153-969-1

AMAZING STORIES™

LUCY MAUD MONTGOMERY

The Incredible Life of the
Creator of Anne of Green Gables

BIOGRAPHY
by Stan Sauerwein

ISBN 1-55153-775-3

by the same author

AMAZING STORIES™

PIERRE ELLIOTT TRUDEAU

The Fascinating Life of Canada's
Most Flamboyant Prime Minister

BIOGRAPHY
by Stan Sauerwein

ISBN 1-55153-945-4

OTHER AMAZING STORIES

These titles are available wherever you buy books. If you have trouble finding the book you want, call the Altitude order desk at **1-800-957-6888**, e-mail your request to: **orderdesk@altitudepublishing.com** or visit our Web site at **www.amazingstories.ca**

New AMAZING STORIES titles are published every month.